The Caring Church

Other Fortress books by Howard W. Stone:

Crisis Counseling
Suicide and Grief

Also,

Coeditor with Howard Clinebell of the *Creative Pastoral Care and Counseling* series (1974–   )

Coeditor with James Duke of Friedrich Schleiermacher's *Christian Caring: Selections from Practical Theology*

The Caring Church

A Guide for Lay Pastoral Care

Howard W. Stone

Fortress Press   Minneapolis

To my colleagues at Brite Divinity School,
who challenge and comfort and provide the
invigorating environment in which I live and work

THE CARING CHURCH
A Guide for Lay Pastoral Care

First Fortress edition 1991. Original paperback edition, *The Caring Church: A Guide for Lay Pastoral Care,* published by Harper and Row Publishers, Inc., copyright © 1983, Howard W. Stone.

Cover photo by Winston Pote from A. Devaney, Inc., N.Y.

Library of Congress Cataloging-in-Publication Data

Stone, Howard W.
    The caring church : a guide for lay pastoral care / Howard W. Stone. — 1st Fortress ed.
      p.   cm.
    Includes bibliographical references.
    ISBN 0-8006-2618-4 (alk. paper)
    1. Lay ministry.   2. Pastoral counseling.   I. Title.
BV677.S86 1991
253—dc20   91-31793
                                                 CIP

Manufactured in the U.S.A.   AF 1-2618
95   94   93   92   91   1   2   3   4   5   6   7   8   9   10

Contents

Preface

The final chapter of a book I wrote nearly twenty years ago discussed preventive pastoral care. In it I suggested somewhat naively that lay people ought to be incorporated into pastoral care. I believed it would be an opportunity for them to "express their Christian concern concretely."[1]

My interest continued after I joined Interfaith Counseling Service in Scottsdale, Arizona, and began to lead workshops for lay people. With the assistance of outside funding and several staff members who taught what we called Befriender Training sessions, my ideas about lay pastoral care developed. The appointment to teach pastoral care and pastoral counseling at Brite Divinity School provided a further impetus to my interest in the area. I encountered many, students and pastors, who were asking, "How do you get such a group going?" "What do you cover in the training sessions?" "How do you select the right people to be trained?"

These and many other questions served to focus my attention on the need for lay ministry. Finally, when my colleague Marcus Bryant and I led a seminar on the subject during an annual convention of the American Association of Pastoral Counselors, I realized that these ideas had come of age. The number and quality of responses at the workshop were astounding, and the interest in lay pastoral care was phenomenal.

Ongoing lay pastoral care groups already exist throughout Canada and the United States, and they are making an impact upon the church. The times are ready for ministers to look to the laity as partners in the pastoral care task. This is occasionally billed as something new—but in truth we are only reincorporating a traditional function of pastoral care that has fallen into disuse.[2] Throughout the centuries laity and clergy have shared the ministry of care. During some eras of church history the work of lay people was more noticeable than in others, but the laity has always offered informal pastoral care in some greater or lesser way.

So why train people in lay pastoral care if they are already doing it? First, it will highlight, bless, and strengthen the care already being offered by the laity. Second, it will increase the confidence of those lay people who desire to care for others but feel themselves lacking in skills or ability. Training in lay pastoral care has the potential to reshape the church's theology and invigorate its existing ministry of care. The concept of "the priesthood of all believers" can thus be put into practice in an extremely vital way.

Among readers who turn to this book, there will be especially two groups—those leaders who are organizing lay training in local parishes, and the trainees who desire to more fully care for others. Each group might wish to read the book somewhat differently. It is suggested that leaders developing a lay pastoral care class read the first three chapters very carefully—particularly chapter 3, which discusses administrative and recruitment matters—before moving on to the following chapters that describe in detail the eight sessions. Those who are attending a lay pastoral care class and using this book as a text may want to read only the introductory chapter (chapter 1) and then skip to chapter 4 for the beginning of the training sessions. At some time during the sessions trainees may wish to return to chapter 2 on the theology of lay ministry to understand more clearly the underpinnings of all that is being taught. The cases used throughout this book are, in all instances, composites of several actual situations and thus are disguised, and all names in these cases have been fictitiously assigned.

I am not able to express appreciation in this brief preface to everyone who assisted me in the work of writing the book. A grant from the Brite Research and Development Fund provided considerable help for the preparation of the manuscript. Thanks are due to Jan Weinberg and Alan Field, who taught a number of befriender groups for Interfaith Counseling Service and tested out many ideas about lay pastoral care. I would also like to thank the readers whose invaluable criticism helps to shape the book's final form: Marcus Bryant, William Clements, Howard Clinebell, William Countryman, James Duke, and Jane McDonald. I owe gratitude to Jean Burnham, Sharlie Tomlinson, and Kay Netlege, who typed numerous drafts of the manuscript, and I am indebted to Jane Lovett for the bibliographical research she completed. And I am especially grateful to Karen Stone, herself a busy artist, art historian, and teacher, who shared her valuable time to assist in the preparation of the manuscript.

Notes on the Revised Edition

Sometimes when you write a book you wonder if there is anyone out there. Except for the comments of a few reviewers nothing is heard. Not so with *The Caring Church.* I have appreciated the responses of the many ministers and lay persons who have used this book. Their insights have helped me in my continuing reflection about lay pastoral care ministry and have allowed me to reshape the training program that is covered in these pages. To all who have written, thank you. Please keep your cards and letters coming. Who knows, maybe there will be a second revision of *The Caring Church!*

Lay pastoral care ministry is alive and well in the church. In fact, it is going on more now than when the book first came out in 1983. When I performed a library search of materials on the topic written since then, I was stunned by the number of doctor of ministry theses on the subject; there were over twenty on some part of lay pastoral care ministry.

I have made minor changes throughout the book, but want here to mention significant changes or additions. Chapter 3 deals with the administration of lay pastoral care programs; as I have heard from pastors and lay persons around the country I have raised more of the actual issues that may be encountered in the development of such a program. I never teach the lay pastoral care program the same way twice; I am always experimenting with ways to improve it. Soon after the first edition of *The Caring Church* hit the bookstores, I had made some changes in session one. I started using cases, and found class members grasping how they could respond to others in the congregation faster than before. So I now always use cases; four of them can be found in appendix C. Some additions were also made in the final two chapters addressing the ongoing work of lay pastoral care teams.

I wish you the best in your lay pastoral care ministries.

1

Pastoral Care and the Ministry of the Laity

Most people in the church knew there was a problem, at least a serious one, when Rebecca Blume's husband, George, started shoving the clerk at the hardware store. George had gone to buy parts for a craft project he was working on and became incensed when the store did not have what he needed. He started yelling at the high school-aged employee: "Your father would have stocked those tacks. He knew what people needed and supplied it for them." The student evidently apologized and stated that his father never owned or worked at the store, but that was not enough to quell Mr. Blume. He started pushing the clerk, a minor tussle.

When George stormed out, he could not find his car. He returned to the store and loudly demanded that they give him back his car. Then he begged for his car, offering them all of his money for it. Finally the manager called the police.

The incident at the hardware store got around town quickly. Evidently, Rebecca was aware that George was not his old self, but she either was trying to hide it or avoid facing that her husband of forty-some years had a problem. She had not allowed George to drive alone for several years because he had become so forgetful, but the morning of the hardware store incident she was visiting a neighbor and returned to find him gone.

Now she had to face it. "George's problem," as she called it, was diagnosed by her physician as a probable case of Alzheimer's disease. Rebecca was devastated. She had seen a television program on Public Broadcasting System on Alzheimer's and knew what lay ahead. Taking care of George by herself had worn her out. George would get up in the middle of the night and roam the house, pacing hour after hour, keeping her awake. In addition, she had her own

11

problems with arthritis. Rebecca was exhausted and frightened. She felt helpless and utterly alone.

From time to time similar situations arise in most churches, cases that nearly all the members become aware of though they are afraid to become involved. A few people in Rebecca's congregation made jokes about what had happened—some even guessed that George had been drinking too much—but most felt sorry for them, even though they were afraid to do anything about it.

Pastor Abramson was very helpful to Rebecca. The two already had a close relationship—they both had served on the worship committee a few years ago—and Rebecca appreciated her concern. With medications George was calmer and sleeping better at night. Nevertheless, the pastor recognized a number of potential problems for Rebecca, since George had Alzheimer's. She put her in touch with a member of the congregation, a bank trust officer, who helped address legal and financial issues that had to be resolved before George got even worse. Pastor Abramson also realized that Rebecca was going to need help around the house and suggested that some of the members of the congregation could give assistance there. Neither the doctors nor Rebecca were ready to put George in an institution immediately, though it was mentioned as a possibility in the future.

Elizabeth Bender also responded. She did not know what to say and felt very uncomfortable, but her neighborliness and her real concern for others won out over her fears. When she heard what had happened, Elizabeth went over to Rebecca's house. She took a casserole and some vegetables for an evening meal. She offered to go shopping for them or stay with George when Rebecca wanted to get out of the house, something she had had little opportunity to do in the last year or so. Elizabeth also asked what other specific things she could do to help.

Elizabeth's reaching out had a powerful impact on Rebecca, who at last broke down under the weight of her load and cried. After some conversation and a cup of tea, Rebecca—first reluctantly, then willingly—agreed to let Elizabeth help out with shopping and later with care for George while she was attending to things away from home.

On several subsequent evenings Elizabeth again took supper to the Blumes, and arranged for other members of the congregation to do likewise. She continued to look for ways in which she could ease Rebecca's situation without being asked and yet without being too intrusive.

Rebecca Blume's problems were certainly not *resolved* by the intervention of these members of her congregation, but Pastor Abramson, the bank trust officer, Elizabeth Bender, and several other individuals moved her toward some temporary solutions to what was likely to be a protracted period of difficulty and let her know she was not alone, that there were people who cared and could be counted on for comfort, support, and help.

I selected the case of Rebecca Blume for this review because I think it serves as an example of what can be accomplished when Christians take seriously the fact that pastoral care is the responsibility of all individuals—to "bear one another's burdens" (Gal. 6:2)—and not only of the ordained clergy.

Situations like Rebecca Blume's do arise in our churches. Individuals develop Alzheimer's disease, marriages break up, people die, children leave home, accidents occur, illnesses strike, jobs are lost, doubts befall, loneliness descends. The pain and struggle in society and in human relationships are not fantasies of a Bergman film; they are part of the experience of each individual and each community of Christians. The burden of responsibility to people in pain, uncertainty, confusion, or need is something we all bear—pastor and lay person alike. In recent years especially, there has been a tendency to lay this responsibility upon the minister's shoulders. "I am not trained to do that sort of thing" or "I don't know what to say" are not just excuses; they are the genuine apprehensions of many people. But the pastor should not and cannot be the only one who cares for others on behalf of the church.

The purpose of this book is to provide some answers to the misgivings of church members, and skills to foster the confidence of lay persons in their ministry to others. It does not represent the only way to train lay people in pastoral care—nor does it even assume that they have to be trained. But it is my experience that many who are admonished in a sermon to "witness" or "help your neighbor" are saying in their minds, "I don't know how." The present task, therefore, is to present a training paradigm that teaches lay people some basic ways of responding to those who suffer.

Pastoral Care in Historical Perspective

Clebsch and Jaekle, in their historically based definition of pastoral care ("helping acts, done by *representative Christian persons,* directed toward the *healing, sustaining, guiding,* and *reconciling* of *troubled persons* whose troubles arise *in the context of ultimate meanings and concerns*"),[1] make the point that the phrase "representative Christian persons" does not refer only to the ordained clergy.

> Such representative persons may or may not hold specific offices in a Christian church. . . . They may hold no churchly office whatever. Yet to perform pastoral care, they must in some way possess and exercise, or be taken to possess and exercise, the resources of the Christian faith, the wisdom distilled from Christians' experiences, and the authority of a company of Christian believers. . . . It is noteworthy that, while the Christian tradition yields abundant literature showing how ordained persons should function as pastors, pastoring by unofficial persons has undergone relatively little thoughtful analysis, although its continual exercise cannot be doubted.[2]

Pastoral care is a task of the total Christian community—a task of ministering to one another and reaching out beyond ourselves. Daniel Day Williams, in defining the church, put it this way: "All the lines of thought we have been exploring lead to one conclusion about the Church: It is the true Christian community holding out hope for the nurture and health of spirit of those within it when it is animated by the spirit of acceptance, of reconciliation, and of service."[3] Another interesting, but ironic, observation was made by Detwiler-Zapp and Dixon, who noted that in most parishes laity teach the church school, lead stewardship drives, do youth work, assist with the maintenance of building and grounds, and lead in worship—while pastoral care is left to the clergy.[4] Yet paradoxically, lay people—specifically because they are lay people, in close daily contact with suffering and alienated persons at their jobs, in their homes, and among their friends—are uniquely suited to be partners with the clergy in the ministry of caregiving. As such, they are a vast and largely unused support system in the contemporary church.

Throughout the centuries, as Clebsch and Jaekle suggest, the laity has always been a part of pastoral care ministry. The emphasis upon such a ministry and the visibility of such caring have varied considerably from era to era. In recent decades lay pastoral care appears to have receded in practice, and when given it is often without the support or encouragement of the ordained.

With the advent of specialization in pastoral counseling has come a growing belief among lay and clergy alike that pastoral care can be performed only by ordained ministers. If all of pastoral care could be summed up as counseling, then I would agree. But if we readopt the traditional, historical tasks of pastoral care—healing, sustaining, guiding, and reconciling—and if we accept our responsibility to care for others as God has loved us, then the lay person is not only able but is *commissioned* to participate.[5]

The need for friendship, emotional support, concern, and advice for individuals, couples, or families who are in the midst of life's crises is undeniable. When stretched to the limit by problems in living, people function poorly as employees on their jobs, as homemakers, as parents, and as couples with each other.

People who experience difficulties are not always willing or able to seek out professional therapy, nor is it always necessary. They are nevertheless in emotional pain and often are more open to outside intervention. Frequently the help that is most easily accepted by someone in emotional distress is that of an acquaintance. Unfortunately, many people who are confronted with someone who has recently lost a husband through death or a wife by divorce, who has a child in trouble with the law or a spouse who drinks excessively, feel uncomfortable or incapable of handling the situation. They respond either by giving advice or by standing on the sidelines wanting very much to help but afraid to get involved. The majority of them have not been trained—nor do they believe themselves to have the skills—to assist in life's crises.

It is crucial to recognize that training lay persons in the caring ministry of the church involves far more than getting a few people to help the minister with visitation. The training creates a place in the life and ministry of the church for those who, hearing and believing, want to put their faith into practice in a tangible way. "Love one another" (John 15:17) becomes something *active*. To quote Marcus Bryant, "There is but one true test of the existence of God's loving spirit among his people—the fruits of the Spirit. In other words, what is the outcome of my being loved and forgiven by God? My response is with my whole self—in terms of who I am, in the kind of relationships I have with others and in service to others."[6]

Obstacles to Lay Pastoral Care Training

At Interfaith Counseling Service in Scottsdale, Arizona, where I worked from 1971 to 1979, lay pastoral care training (we called it Befriender Training) was offered at more than seventy local churches. Some two thousand people were trained. As more and more churches participated in the training program, some complications developed. In addition to the normal difficulties of fine-tuning a training program so that it would function effectively, the complications arose from the clergy's reservations and the laity's reactions to lay pastoral care. Strong negative reactions from either side can greatly hinder such a ministry, and when both are negative a successfully organized training group in lay pastoral care will be next to impossible to achieve. Through talks with other pastors who have trained people in lay caregiving and from my personal experiences in Arizona and Texas, I have become aware of some possible hindrances to effective lay participation in pastoral ministry. A little forethought and learning from others' experiences can help the reader avoid or ease the following problems.

Congregational Attitudes

Gossip is a favorite pastime in some churches. Its natural product is a hesitancy on the part of people to talk openly about their difficulties—especially if those difficulties are emotionally loaded, as in the case related at the beginning of this chapter. People selected to serve as carers obviously cannot be meddling characters, or the best of training will prove worthless.

There is an expectation or even a demand for specialization, especially in middle- to upper-middle-class, highly educated congregations. The pastor is clearly the specialist, and lay people are viewed as less capable or incapable of rendering effective care in crises. But if Jesus' command to "love your neighbor" is relegated only to the professional Christian, lay pastoral care will founder.

A "that's-what-we-pay-'em-for" attitude can also inhibit lay pastoral care. The minister is paid to do ministry. Pastoral care is a chief part of that ministry; therefore, why ask lay people to do it? Such an attitude occurs when members of the congregation are busy at their own jobs and with their own lives, and do not have time to "do someone else's job."

Most pastors have been out of town at some time when an active church member experienced adversity. After the crisis passed and the pastor returned home it may be that the church member said, "I understand why you couldn't be there"—but did not totally understand or even forgive. It is a fact that most people want the *pastor* when there is a serious crisis such as death or illness. Some may even worry that if lay people respond first in a time of crisis, that the pastor might not come; therefore, when lay pastoral care is suggested they fear that the pastor will be less available. On the contrary: lay ministry is not a replacement for the pastor's care but an *addition* and an enrichment to it.

Clergy Reactions

Most pastors see themselves as shepherds who are there to do whatever is needed for their flocks. It follows that in their minds *they* are the ones to do the serving, rather than the ones to train others to serve. This tends to make them poor sharers or delegators of the lay pastoral care task.

Reluctance to share the pastoral care task occurs partly because ministers are so action-oriented. This clergy barrier to lay pastoral care arises out of ministers' deep concern for the people they serve. According to Detwiler-Zapp and Dixon,

> Crisis situations intensify one's natural desire to act. . . . Spontaneous, immediate action on the part of the pastor can unintentionally inhibit those in crisis from using personal resources, prevent them from calling on available support from family or friends, and increase their feelings of inadequacy. The result is an exhausted helper and a discouraged, dependent person ill-equipped to meet the next crisis. The inclination and ability to act quickly could prevent a pastor from recognizing an opportunity to use the talents, life experiences, and caregiving skills of many church members.[7]

Another clergy reaction is based on pastors' beliefs about lay people. Since the church is a volunteer organization, many ministers know they do not have the same control over lay volunteers that they would have over paid employees. Out of frustration and bitter experience some pastors have avoided sharing pastoral care with the laity because "you can't be sure if they'll really make the visit." There is a mixture of reality and sour grapes in this reaction. Although one cannot depend on others as well as one can on oneself, it is important to share the responsibility. To be sure, it must be done with wisdom and good administrative planning— but it is vital that it be done, because caring for the neighbor is the very essence of the body of Christ.

Finally, some ministers see pastoral care as the most self-nourishing thing they can do. It is difficult to receive emotional and spiritual sustenance from administrative duties—or even, to some, from preaching. What personally rewarding activities remain for ministers but pastoral care?

Certainly there are other beliefs and reactions that hinder pulpit or pew from involvement in effective lay pastoral care. I have found the ones listed above in a significant number of situations and suggest them as areas of concern. Ironically, in the training we offered in Arizona, fully half of the pastors had no desire to use trained lay pastoral carers as a part of the visitation ministry of the church. A number of them were "too busy" with more important things (frequently their own pastoral care visits) or seemed threatened by the idea of sharing their pastoral duties. In one case the pastor did not want the congregation's trainees to visit the sick or shut-in but told them, "Since now you're good at talking to people, you can be every-member visitors for our stewardship program." (That time, I was angry.) As a rule, if a pastor can nondefensively accept lay participation in pastoral care and administer it effectively over a period of time, the congregation will be able to accept it as well. If the pastor is ambivalent, the program usually will not get off the ground or, if started, will meet an early death. Time and time again this has borne out to be true.

Lay Pastoral Care in the Parish

There are in this world an abundance of people who cry for help and need to be served. At the same time, an abundance of Christians have a need to express their love. My vision for lay pastoral care is that a core of individuals from local parishes be trained in caring skills. I would like to see ongoing groups established in churches whereby troubled people, the recently bereaved, shut-ins, nursing home residents, and the unchurched could be visited in a systematic way. Not everyone who is trained in lay pastoral care could or would take part in such a group, but they should be given the opportunity to do so.

Lay pastoral care does not require an ongoing group or structure in order to function. In fact, much effective pastoral care is already being offered by people who have never had any training at all! The purpose of the training is to enhance and recognize the pastoral ministry already being given by lay persons and to assist others who want to do more but are uncertain about how to go about it. The training is a vehicle to assist their ministry and is not an end in itself.

Design of the Book

The Caring Church is offered to assist the reentry of lay persons into the historical functions of pastoral care in the church. The following chapter will discuss a theological understanding of lay pastoral care ministry. Chapter 3 addresses the nitty-gritty task of setting up such a program in a local church and deals with a number of specific planning and administrative matters. Chapters 4–11 detail an eight-session training model. They offer a suggested program that can be adapted by leaders and participants to fit the needs of each church, group, and individual. Finally, chapter 12 will highlight the major steps of the training paradigm and point to possible future directions that lay pastoral care can take when a church has completed such a class and established an ongoing group.

The training of lay people can be a time-consuming task as well as a very enriching experience. No one church will ever attain the ideal of what lay pastoral care could be, but clergy and lay persons can work side by side in a very satisfying way—a way in which they can hear and respond to the Word as it is encountered in their daily lives.

2

Lay Pastoral Care from a Theological Perspective

I have often been moved by the answer to the first question in *The Westminster Shorter Catechism,* which asks, "What is our chief end?" The response beautifully expresses the joy of our redeemed relationship with God: "Our chief end is to glorify God, and to enjoy God forever."

A New Relationship in Christ

The foundation of the new life transformed by Christ's suffering and resurrection—and our primary reason for glorifying God—is justification by faith. Through the incarnation in Christ, God has inaugurated new life and called us into an intimate relationship. This reconciled relationship liberates us from all concern over gaining our salvation or even doing what is right to please God. We are free persons. God wants it that way and does not intend that we do anything to achieve this relationship but offers it freely, as a gift. It is an exciting and joyful thing!

Not only are we free from worry over making ourselves right with God and from long lists of "do's and don'ts" ruling our lives, but our fears, anxieties, and energies are loosed to be channeled into appreciating, honoring, even *enjoying* God, as the *Westminster Catechism* so perfectly claims. In the midst of the suffering and uncertainty of this life there is one who is certain, and upon whom we can rely.

Luther commented on the new life in Christ, "A Christian is a perfectly free lord of all, subject to none. A Christian is a perfectly

21

dutiful servant of all, subject to all."[1] Our Christ-relationship does not exempt us from good works, as Luther pointed out, but rather from false understandings of them, from needless attempts to gain salvation through anything we can do. As Paul Althaus has written, "Christian behavior, therefore, however imperfect and sinful it may be in and of itself, is good because it is grounded in the assurance of a prior 'yes', in that divine approval which the Christian does not have to seek because it has already been given. This is why the Christian can go ahead and act in confidence and joy, even though his works are still impure and imperfect."[2]

Martin Luther explained the interrelationship of love of God and love of neighbor by comparing it to a water fountain. His image shows God's love flowing into us and then flowing out to our neighbor. Faith, which accepts God's love coming to us, and love of neighbor, which passes on, are part of the same process. Althaus contends,

> Because the Christian's activity flows out of his experience of God's love and since this activity is in itself love, it shares all the characteristics of God's own love. God wants his people to act spontaneously, freely and voluntarily, happily and eagerly. Where the Spirit and faith do their work, the Christian does not respond compulsively or artificially to his neighbor; rather, he acts with an inner necessity comparable to the natural processes by which trees bear fruit.[3]

This is the task of all Christians and the natural fruit of our redeemed life in Christ: to care for those who are near us. It is not only the responsibility of the ordained; the ministry of caring for our neighbor is one in which we are all participants.

Love of Neighbor

To comprehend better what the new Testament meant by love of neighbor, let us examine it briefly. The law of love, also referred to as the love command or the love ethic and expressed in such phrases as "love your neighbor," "love your brothers and sisters," "love one another," or even "love your enemy," is most clearly portrayed in the Synoptics, in Paul's letters, and in John.

The double command to love God and neighbor is found in all three Synoptic Gospels (Matt. 22:34-40, Mark 12:28-34, and Luke 10:25-37), but in Matthew (5:43-48) and Luke (6:27-36) the love ethic is radicalized; we are told to love our *enemies*. The following discussion will review all of the above texts and will examine Reformation insights in the recapturing of these biblical views.[4]

Synoptic Gospels

In the time of Christ, rabbis were frequently challenged to sum up the 613 commandments of the law. The scribe in Mark's version of the double command (12:28-34) makes such a request of Jesus, apparently in a nonabrasive way. He is told by Jesus that to love God and neighbor are the quintessence of the law. To love one's neighbor and to love God are treated as belonging to a class apart from all the other commandments; each is an integral part of the *chief commandment*. It is interesting to observe in Matthew's version (22:34-40) that the questioner is a lawyer rather than a scribe and that his question is phrased to "test" Jesus, to put him on the spot. Matthew's account of Jesus' response also emphasizes the relatedness of the two commands (22:38-39). Love of God is put forth as the "great and first commandment" but love of neighbor is "like" it. He goes on to say that "all the law and the prophets" depend on the double command (22:40).

Both Matthew's and Mark's reports of the double command to love God and neighbor emphasize the supreme importance of *both* commandments—which would in effect delimit the significance of the ceremonial laws of the time (especially among the scribes and Pharisees) and elevate the importance of caring for one's neighbors.

In Luke's discussion of the double command it is crucial, for an understanding of love of neighbor, to include the parable of the Good Samaritan that follows it (6:30-37). With priest and Levite refusing to help while a hated Samaritan gives assistance, Jesus' parable emphasizes that simply knowing what is right is insufficient. Action is required, and obedience to the law of love breaks down artificial boundaries of sex, age, caste, nation, or race. Furnish comments on the parable:

> Obedience in love establishes relationships where none were conceivable or possible before. Thus, the problem of neighbor is not one of definition but of performance, and where there is performance, where one's deeds are moved and shaped by love, there is neither time nor reason to ask, "*Who* is my neighbor?" . . . Concrete deeds of love, not casuistic definitions of love's limits, should be of concern.[5]

Both love of God and love of neighbor are inextricably linked parts of one and the same response to God's grace and to God's claim upon our lives. To love one's neighbor is to love God; Christ said, "As you did it to one of the least of these . . . you did it to me" (Matt. 25:40). The symbiosis between the two is expressed, in one way or another, in each of the Synoptics. We owe to our neighbor the same selfless love that we undeservedly receive from God and gratefully return in worship, in prayer, and in love to our neighbor.

Paul

The law of love is also articulated in the writings of Paul (although there are no explicit parallels to the double command as found in the Synoptics).[6] The love ethic of Paul is stated from the viewpoint of his "theology of the cross." According to Paul, Christ is no mere prophet or teacher; in his life, death, and resurrection he is the very embodiment of the promise that God had been acting out with the children of Israel, throughout antiquity—the promise of redemption and new life. At the same time he embodies the new law: to give oneself totally in the service of love.

Since believing in Christ is not to assent to a dogma but to be joined with him and to become a participant in his suffering, death, and resurrection, the Christian is thereby released from the bondage of desire and self-will and is instead bound by the freedom of God's grace to serve and care for others.

John

A key to understanding the law of love as revealed in the Gospel of John is provided by the "farewell discourses" (chapters 13–17). In this section of John the emphasis is on love within the Christian community: "By this love you have for one another, everyone will know that you are my disciples" (13:35). Serving others, noted in the Synoptics and Paul, is here transformed into discipleship. We are to follow Christ's example—"you also should do as I have done to you" (13:15). The high point of the thirteenth chapter of John articulates the author's understanding of Christ's law of love: "A new commandment I give to you, that you love one another" (13:34). The shackles of the old law are broken and there is a new law; following Christ means emptying oneself, serving and caring for others within the community.

The Reformers

The theology of the Reformation was strongly directed by the law of love and service to one's neighbor. To paraphrase Martin Luther, a Christian lives in Christ through faith and in the neighbor through love. By faith the Christian is caught up beyond oneself into God. By love, the Christian sinks down beneath oneself into the neighbor.[7]

According to Luther, it is inevitable that a stream of loving service should flow from the spring of a life redeemed by and committed to Christ—who told us he "came not to be served but to serve" (Mark 10:45). Luther's only concern was that Christians should avoid the error of, on the one hand, releasing the bonds of love's law or, on the other hand, binding the free, redemptive act—God's gift of grace received through faith.

The double command of love found in the Synoptics is molded into one by Luther. He maintains that any love we have for God is properly offered to others. Thus, he contends, in the suffering and needy neighbor we find and love God; we serve the neighbor whenever we want to serve God; "Thus the commandment to love God is fully and completely subsumed in the commandment to love our neighbor."[8]

Our responsibility as Christians to love and serve others is in spite of the inherent limitedness of our response in faith. Though the bondage of sin and alienation has been broken in Christ, we are each still "both saint and sinner," and all attempts at loving others—including pastoral care (with or without the benefit of a training course)—will remain fragile and sometimes weak. Rather than becoming discouraged by these realities, Luther urges, we should remind ourselves of Christ's command to go, serve, and care, with the assurance that our liberation, meted out by Christ through his power, gives us the capability of caring for others.

It is vital to add that God does not expect all Christians to obey the law of love in the same way. As Luther writes, "It is God's firm intention that all the saints are to live in the same faith, and be moved and guided by the same Spirit; but in external matters carry out different works."[9] In Luther, then, the love command is not confused with redemption but is seen as the natural response of the Christian to the neighbor, taking on various forms of service depending on the needs of the other and the talents of the Christian.

Summing up some of the major themes from Paul, the Gospel authors, and the reformers, let me suggest nine points that can serve as a foundation for the pastoral care we offer.

1. Our ministry of loving and caring for others is based on our prior acceptance and love by God. God welcomes us back into a right relationship (reconciles us) and frees us to serve. All care for others flows out from God's love for us.

2. In this new relationship the old law is replaced by the *law of love*. Caring for God and neighbor becomes the criterion by which our actions are assessed. This does not mean that the old law has no import, but that it must be weighed against the law of love. Luther explains, "In all his works he should be guided by this thought and look to this one thing alone, that he may serve and benefit others in all that he does, having regard to nothing except the need and advantage of his neighbor."[10]

3. One way to love God is to love one's neighbor. God would sooner have us invest our time and energy in serving our neighbor than in spending extensive amounts of time on acts of worship or scrupulous introspection. To quote Luther again: "God would much rather be deprived of his service than of the service you owe your neighbor."[11] This in no way demeans the worship, honor, and "enjoyment" of God or the Christian's sense of awe and wonder in God's presence; but it recognizes that service to our sisters and brothers is a central feature of our life "in Christ."

4. The love and care we address to others is given to other Christians (especially as seen in John), to those who are not members of the Christian community "whether Jew or Greek," and even to our enemies. Kierkegaard, discussing love of others, defined neighbor by saying that if there are only two people, the other person is the neighbor; "If there are millions, each one of these is the neighbor."[12]

5. Luther's analogy of the love of God channeled through us as through a fountain emphasizes that we can be used to carry God's love to others. (It is not something we control but is dependent on the Spirit.) On such occasions our care is transformed and we become Christ for the other.

6. Each member of the Christian community has a different configuration of gifts. (The "affirming your own gifts" exercise in the first meeting of the training program will amply bear this out. See chapter 4.) All of us have a responsibility to use those particular

talents that we have been given. We are not to covet others' gifts but rather enhance and use our own unique talents to their fullest extent.

7. Love of neighbor is not just the correct attitude or the right belief. It is not simply knowing what to do or feeling affection and compassion. It is all of these, but it is also *action*—faith, active in love.

8. Pastoral care is a task to which we have been charged; we are *commanded* to love others, no matter how difficult that might be. Although we love each other freely, spontaneously, and in gratitude to God for God's grace toward us, our Christian freedom does not allow us to sit down on the job.

9. The law of love, to serve our neighbor, is a responsibility of the whole community of faith. Pastoral care as an expression of love for the neighbor is not reserved for the ordained but is the duty of all who have been transformed by God's redemptive love. Although there may be other distinctions between professional clergy and laity, in this respect we are all "professionals" in Christ.

Ministry and the Laity

A number of churches have begun the practice of listing their staff on the Sunday bulletin in the following manner:

Ministers: All of the members of the congregation
Pastor: Rev. Jane Doe
Organist: (etc.)

If such a statement is overly cute and probably ignored, at least it acknowledges the fact that the laity shares in its ministry. Let us briefly explore the place of lay people in the ministry of the church.

The need to understand the laity's place in the church would not have been a major issue in the church of New Testament times. Although a precise picture of what the church was like in the first century cannot be drawn, it is quite clear that there were no sharp divisions between clergy and laity.[13] Alan Richardson, commenting on the New Testament ethos, writes that a lay person, i.e., a member of the *laos,* is not like the modern understanding of

> a church member who has no ministerial responsibility, one who has handed over [the] functions of evangelism and pastoral care to certain professional Christians who are paid to perform them. All the laity

. . . if we use the term in the biblical way, are priests and ministers of the Church of Jesus Christ; and all the 'ministers', are equally lay [persons].[14]

This point is dramatically emphasized when the Greek text of 1 Peter 2:9 is viewed: "But you are a chosen race, a royal priesthood, a holy nation, God's own people, that you may declare the wonderful deeds of him who called you out of darkness into his marvelous light." The word used for "people" here is *laos*—laity.

This relative lack of distinction between clergy and laity began to erode soon after the New Testament authors had blotted the ink on their manuscripts. Just where and when the change occurred is hard to document with precision, for it was an evolution. With the passage of time, an increasingly greater differentiation between clergy and laity developed, a distinction that was to become an issue in the Reformation.

The sixteenth-century reformers argued that ministry is for all people in the church, not just a special class. Two of Luther's predominant themes were vocation or calling (one's station in life), and the priesthood of all believers (which is actually contained within Luther's understanding of vocation)—ideas which helped the church of that time to understand ministry. I believe they can help us today. To comprehend better what the ministry of the laity as well as clergy should be at present, we are obliged to review these two concepts very briefly.

One's Station in Life

The first vocation of Christians, as Luther speaks of it, is the state (lot, status, station, office) in which we find ourselves. Paul, in the seventh chapter of First Corinthians, mentions several of these states (verses 17-24), and suggests we should be able to accept whatever unchangeable life situations we find ourselves in. Luther included in this first type of vocation one's *occupation* (teacher, seamstress, poet, engineer, firefighter), one's *status* (single, husband, wife, child), or one's *place in life* (rich, poor, blind, sighted). This calling includes our everyday tasks, our occupations, our studies, and so on. In this regard, Stuempfle suggests every Christian, no matter what one's office or status in church or world, lives out one's life under God's call. "Each could equally be the place of service to the neighbor, and thus to God. Luther, I think, would have liked the man who, when asked by a perfervid evangelist what he did to serve the Lord, responded without blinking an eye: 'I bake bread.' "[15]

Luther argued from his understanding of Paul in First Corinthians that every station in life is equal, and there is no one status higher than another. As he claimed, "The housemaid on her knees scrubbing the floor is doing a work as pleasing in the eyes of Almighty God as the priest on his knees before the altar saying the mass."[16] We are called to perform our daily tasks as best we can in whatever of life's situations we find ourselves, realizing that in that particular place we can minister to those around us.[17]

The Priesthood of All Believers

The second vocation or calling of every Christian is as a member of the priesthood of all believers. Under the Mosaic covenant all the people of Israel were to be a "kingdom of priests" (Exod. 19:6 ff., Lev. 11:44 ff., Num. 15:40, Isa. 61:6). God is a holy God; and since human holiness is imperfect, the people of Israel needed someone to intercede for them before God. That was the function of the High Priest—mediating between God and the people.

In the New Testament the terms *priesthood* or *priest* do not refer to the office of ministry. First Corinthians 12:28 ff. and Ephesians 4:11 ff. contain lists of offices and responsibilities in the church but do not mention priests. In the New Testament there are references to only two types of Christian priesthood: the priesthood of Christ (Heb. 6:20; 7:26 ff.) and the universal priesthood (1 Pet. 2:9; Rev. 5:10).

Wilkens describes Luther's understanding of the second vocation with great clarity:

> It is a calling with, so to speak, both vertical and horizontal dimensions. Vertically, the calling grants the privilege of free access to God with the potential of faith and salvation. Horizontally, the calling occasions the responsibility of sharing the Gospel through concrete priestly functions or ministries of the Word. These are ministries of love of the first order. Yet there is another aspect of this horizontal dimension of loving ministry; that is, meeting not only one's fellow-priest with the spiritual ministries of the Word but also one's neighbor—fellow-priest or not—in love within the total context of [one's] temporal situation and human need.[18]

To clarify further Luther's recapturing of the original understanding of laity in what he understood as the vocation of the
universal priesthood, let us look at four consequences of his
thinking.

First, the phrase *priesthood of all believers* simply advances the
view that every Christian is ordained as a minister in Christ's
church. Priestly functions such as evangelism, visiting the sick
and lonely, giving spiritual counsel, praying with the dying and
comforting the bereaved, or speaking the word of forgiveness are
not reserved for the clergy. To quote Luther: "Let [every Christian]
be assured of this, that we are all equally priests, that is to say,
we have the same power in respect to the word and the
sacraments."[19]

The second critical observation of Luther was that we are initiated into the priesthood by the washing of baptism—"Through
baptism we have all been ordained as priests."[20] Baptism is the
entrance into the community of faith because of Christ's act of
suffering, death, and resurrection (see Rom. 6:3 ff.), and it is also
the ordination into universal priesthood. The sprinkling of water,
not the donning of a stole, is the rite that makes every Christian
a minister of Christ's church.

Third, the primary task of the priest is to *mediate.* In the Old
Testament the priest stood before God and interceded for the twelve
tribes. On the cross Christ, the new high priest, stood before God
and interceded for us. In the same manner we, when we go to our
neighbor in love, intercede as Christ has done for us. Thus Luther
describes us, when we mediate with our neighbor, as "little
Christs." His intention was not to disestablish priests but to expand
their number to include every Christian.

Fourth, in addition to the tasks of mediating, there are a variety
of ways in which the role of priest or minister to others can be
fulfilled. Whereas each Christian is a member of the royal priesthood, it would lead to chaos if all were involved in the *public*
preaching of the Word or administration of the sacraments. For
this reason the church calls and ordains certain members of the
universal priesthood to serve the functions of public ministry.
Clergy and laity differ only in function; they are not separate orders.
Luther therefore saw the Christian—any Christian—as one who
hears confessions, shares burdens, consoles, prays, listens, visits
the bereaved, gives assurance of forgiveness, and performs other

tasks of ministry. Calvin required the visitation of homes to be carried out not only by the pastor but also by the elders. This certainly goes beyond a contemporary understanding of the laity's role, into many areas that have since been relegated to the clergy. In all likelihood most Christians—lay and clergy alike—would not quarrel with the notion of lay ministry, whether that means involvement in acts of love toward others or a sharing in the universal priesthood of the church. If the ideas presented in this chapter were to be preached on a Sunday morning, most of the congregation assembled would probably nod their heads in agreement. Why, then, do we have to be reminded of our duty as Christians? There appears to be a discrepancy between what Christians think and what they do. As noted elsewhere, one reason is a reticence on the part of some clergy, and even some lay persons, to recognize and encourage church members in pastoral care. Likewise there has been reluctance, lack of confidence, and even fear on the part of lay persons as they consider putting their faith into action in the form of a neighbor-loving pastoral care ministry.

All Christians have two callings, or vocations. The first is to their station in life; the second is to the universal priesthood. In these callings they are commissioned to love and serve others. Pastoral care is a ministry that encompasses much of what we do for our neighbor. It is one way in which God's love is transmitted to those close at hand and those who are not so close.

The training of laity in pastoral care methods is designed to answer fears, give skills and methods, heighten awareness of the task, and above all instill confidence and the conviction that even the most simple acts of caring are commissioned by God. It is a way to assist lay persons in becoming active responders to God's love and can provide an easily grasped means for unleashing their love of others. Lay pastoral care training assists all Christians to share in the ministry to which they have been called.

3

A Training Model
for Getting Started

When a congregation undertakes the training of its laity in pastoral care, it enters a challenging arena of lay involvement in the life and ministry of the church. Planning, administering, recruiting, surveying needs, and teaching the course is a considerable task—more extensive, certainly, than a usual adult education seminar. Therefore, the leader must decide if a rather significant commitment to promote, teach, and support a lay ministry can be made. An alternative requiring less effort is to begin by teaching listening skills, following the outline for the first four sessions. If interest persists, additional training that incorporates the second half of the program described herein may be undertaken.

There are a number of planning and administrative matters that must be considered in preparation for lay pastoral care training. This chapter will discuss several of the more crucial issues. As with all of the ideas in the book, they should be taken only as suggestions and must be adapted to fit each local setting. Furthermore, there are many components other than those listed here that could be helpful. Each time I have taught the lay pastoral care course, I have handled it a little differently. One can never be fully satisfied; compromises will be necessary, and there will not be time to cover everything you would like to cover. Each leader has an understanding of what is best for her or his group's needs and is urged to shape an individualized lay pastoral care training program to suit those particular needs—adding to or deleting from these suggestions as necessary, even while training is in process.

Recruitment

Finding the right volunteers for the first batch of trainees to a great extent determines how well the lay pastoral caring will be received by each congregation. There are several ways in which lay pastoral carers can be selected for inclusion in the training group:

□ The training can be *announced to the whole congregation,* with an invitation to anyone who signs up for the course to attend.

□ It can be a *"by invitation only" group* that is totally selected by the pastor or a lay pastoral care committee.

□ An *existing group* (such as evangelism committee, board of deacons, social ministry group, outreach committee, etc.) can be enlisted for the first group of trainees.

Any of the above methods, or others, may be used. If a good ongoing committee or group does not exist, it is frequently best to advertise the training to the total congregation but do most of the recruitment by personal invitation to members who are especially well suited to be lay pastoral carers.

The training program described herein is not designed for the elite of the church but is one in which almost everyone can participate. It is not only for those who fit the "new mental health ethic" (warm, open, honest, etc.) but is also for tense, shy, or lonely people. Nevertheless, it is possible to make some generalizations about the ideal first training group.

A major criterion is *accessibility.* Do the individuals have the time and willingness to let their routines be occasionally interrupted by the needs of others? Another standard is *stability;* people who are so engrossed in their own problems, pains, or transitions that they will have difficulty hearing another's cares are not good candidates. Third, the church will greatly benefit by training a *heterogeneous* group of lay people: young and old, women and men, those who work outside the home and those who do not, cultural and racial minorities (if they exist in the congregation) and majorities.

Frequently the people first selected are the very empathetic, "giving," tender types of people—and they certainly are needed. But do not forget (how do I say this?) the hard-driving, aggressive, businessperson types. This group is especially skilled at problem-solving and at mobilizing people to take action (whereas the former group is especially gifted at listening and feeling with others' pain). Each personality can learn from the strengths of the other.

Members of church or outside self-help organizations (such as Alcoholics Anonymous) are also valuable participants in such a class. They not only bring expertise to a specialized need area, such as alcoholism, but frequently they are more geared toward assertively caring for others than is the general populace. And it is helpful as well to have a nurse or other employee of a nursing home or hospital to help interpret ministry in those settings.

One caution: be wary of the "church gossip." I do not know a graceful way to keep such a person out of the training group—but if you can, more power to you. *Maintaining confidentiality is crucial,* and no congregation will accept lay pastoral care if secrets are spread throughout the church. One suggestion I have for propitiously using people who have a tendency toward rumor is to give them extracongregational responsibilities—for example, shut-in, nursing home, or neighborhood visits with persons who are not church members. In this way the well-meaning but excessively talkative person can find a personal ministry, and potential problems within the congregation can be avoided.

It has been my experience that most people who are not desirable as lay pastoral carers for one reason or another will select themselves out during the training program. The advantage of having the leader do the major part of the recruitment personally is that he or she will try not to select anyone who might hinder the fledgling lay pastoral care program.

Size of Group

A group of eight to thirty is optimal for the training program described herein. When the group is much smaller than seven or eight, it can be frightening for some individuals and can take on the character of a therapy group—which decidedly is not the purpose of this training (though it may be the aim of some other lay pastoral care training methods, especially those modeled after clinical pastoral education). In some congregations ten class members is more than could be recruited. I have trained groups as small as four with success. When the group gets larger than twenty-five or thirty, it is impossible to offer personal attention to all of the members.

Commitment to Attend All Sessions

The training group is closed-ended, usually lasting eight sessions. It is recommended that all who participate agree to attend every session if at all possible. This requirement is explained during recruitment and at the first session. Those who find that the first class meeting is not their "cup of tea" can drop out. Even after they have committed themselves to the eight sessions, if some individuals appear uncertain about the class or cannot complete the training because of time or other limitations, they should be allowed to leave gracefully. On the other hand, it is occasionally necessary to reassure one who wants to withdraw that the leader believes he or she is doing a creditable job and will undoubtedly make a good lay pastoral carer.

It may be helpful, if this book is being used as a text for the trainees, to request that they all read chapters 1 and 4 prior to the first session. This can provide them with some preparation and a basic understanding of their mission as caregivers.

At the close of the eighth session class members decide if they wish to participate in the organized lay pastoral care ministry (that is, be part of an ongoing group called upon by the pastor to visit others) or if their lay pastoral care is to remain only among those whom they encounter in their day-to-day lives. This decision at the end of the training (but explained during recruitment and in the first session) further allows people to select their level of participation.

Teaching Methods

The following are five different time sequences in which the course has been offered: (1) ten to twelve Sunday morning classes; (2) three all-day Saturday programs; (3) one or two all-day Saturday sessions; (4) a weekend retreat with five or six weekday evening sessions; and (5) eight weekday classes, preferably in the evening.

Sunday mornings are so crowded with activities that they are generally not a good training time; usually more than eight Sunday sessions would be required, and it is difficult to get all of the class members to come regularly for ten to twelve sessions, although it is recognized that at some parishes (like downtown churches) Sunday is the only available time. The Saturday arrangement is quite good, especially if people will commit three or four Saturdays. But that is a big "if" in many congregations and the soccer game or a business trip can get in the way. A weekend retreat may be an ideal arrangement—especially in large churches where the entire class and one of the pastors can be absent for several days.

You probably know by now how well members of your church attend weekend retreats and can decide if that is a viable format.

The most generally useful method (and the arrangement this book describes) is eight weekday sessions, two or two-and-a-half hours duration, generally offered in the evening. Obviously, however, each church will have to adopt a pattern of training that is applicable to its own setting and its members.

As was previously noted, if time does not allow the full eight-week training program, which is the highest recommended format, the course can be shortened to four or five sessions, eliminating the last sessions of the model described herein and using the latter part of the final session as a time to wrap up the course.

Nursing Home Visitation

In order that class members not be limited to discussing and practicing methods of lay pastoral care only hypothetically, they are all given a chance to make actual pastoral care visits. Then, learning becomes very real. Fears have a chance to surface and to be lived with, discussed, and (one hopes) diminished. Confidence is the gain that comes with making these visits, and "I don't know what to say" gives way to "I really *can* do it!"

At the close of the fourth session, each class member is assigned to two or three people to visit in the following two weeks. It is essential during recruitment and in the first class session to alert the group to the fact that they will be making such visits. Class members should not be in for a surprise at the close of the fourth session.

A nursing home has been selected as the suggested ideal setting, initially so that these first "real" visits will be with people who are reasonably easy to visit and greatly appreciative. But there is a long-range benefit to these that may prove to be even more important. Ministry to the lonely and forgotten aged is tragically overlooked; their suffering is a problem of staggering proportions. The church has a responsibility to reach out to elderly shut-ins and nursing home residents all year long, not only at Christmas.

The chaplain or another employee familiar with the nursing home's residents can help select individuals who would welcome a visit. Since some people in a nursing home do not want or cannot profit from a visit, please make certain the contact person at the nursing home really selects *only* those who will benefit from a visit. In several instances when I had not checked this out carefully, "problem" residents were dumped on the unsuspecting lay caller. Class members are not assigned to visit the nursing home residents for only the duration of the training period, they are urged to continue the contacts as long as they are wanted. Such visits can become a very important outreach ministry to a group of people who are seldom visited by people from the outside.

The visits take place individually or in pairs. My recommendation is that most lay pastoral carers make their visits alone, although if the church already has some experienced lay carers, they can be helpful during the first few visits as models. Also, a trainee who is very timid can team up with a more poised class member initially. However, the best learning occurs when every trainee eventually makes the nursing home visits alone.

Confidentiality

In the church it sometimes is difficult to know how much one should talk about another member of the congregation. When troubles befall, troubled individuals may have no difficulty letting others know. In fact they want them to know, and often request their prayers and visits. Others, however, do not want anyone to know; to allow prayer chain members to know that they have a difficulty of any sort would be very distressful for these people. "Bearing one another's burdens" aside, they want to be anonymous in their grief.

The extent to which lay pastoral care volunteers are allowed to talk among themselves as well as out in the congregation should be determined before training begins. The following are a few guidelines that can be used to shape a church's approach to confidentiality.

Silence never should be maintained between lay pastoral carer and pastor in situations where there is a threat of child abuse, danger to another, suicide, homicide, or threat to the life of the president or other public figure. In such cases the caregiver should immediately contact the pastor or leader. In all other instances, the ethics of confidentiality dictate that one not repeat information learned from conversations with a person receiving care. Lay pastoral carers should treat such knowledge as privileged information much as a physician with patient or a psychologist with client. On the other hand, if the person gives permission for what is said to be made public *and* it appears that the information will not damage anyone in any way, then it is permissible to share such information with others.

When the lay pastoral care givers gather to discuss the work they are doing it is appropriate to talk about cases much in the way mental health workers discuss cases, but *what is said in the group must not go outside it, not even to spouses.* However, when the lay caregivers are given an especially sensitive case they should be advised not to discuss the case even in group meetings or individually with other members of the group, but to report back only to the leader.

Lay Leadership

If the lay pastoral care course is being taught by the congregation's pastor, it is required in order to facilitate lay "ownership" of the new care ministry that a lay leader be chosen, preferably before the course begins, so that he or she can assist in the planning and organization of the training program and the ongoing group. After training is completed, the lay leader will serve as a liaison between the pastor and other lay pastoral carers. The exact relationship will depend upon how the two negotiate their roles and responsibilities.

Two crucial matters are to be determined. First, how will people who are to be visited be assigned—by the pastor directly, or by the lay leader, or sometimes one way and sometimes another? A second issue is accountability and feedback after lay pastoral carers are assigned visits. How does one know whether or not a visit has been carried out? Are postcards filled out and returned to the leader, or is he or she to be telephoned? How is important information relayed (such as when a person is near death and wishes the pastor to visit with the Eucharist)? Do people give information directly to the pastor or to the lay leader or to both? How does one know which lay pastoral carers are overloaded with assignments and which have no one to visit? How can consultation be offered when needed by the lay ministers without requiring massive amounts of time on the telephone?

All of these questions will need to be answered, as many as possible before training begins. A number of the solutions may have to be fine-tuned by the school of hard knocks. Pastor, lay leader, and lay pastoral carers must be forthright in giving feedback and criticism from the start so that wrinkles can be ironed out. It will take some time to learn which lay carers are reticent to offer input and ask for help (and will require pursuing) and which ones will want to chat for hours on end about relatively unimportant matters. It is usually most efficient to make the lay pastoral carers responsible for calling the leader or pastor, rather than the other way around.

Help in finding answers to several of the above questions can be found by creating a questionnaire. This instrument can show the pastor and lay leader which areas of lay pastoral care the trainees are willing to undertake (such as evangelism calling, hospital visitation, shut-in visits, grief or dying calls, other crisis situations, etc.), time constraints, types of people they are especially geared to help (such as an AA member seeing an alcoholic or a divorcee seeing someone who is going through a divorce), as well as any types of situations into which they would prefer not to enter.

The Ongoing Lay Pastoral Care Group

One of the goals for lay pastoral care in most churches is not only to train people to care for those they naturally meet in their daily work, recreation, and home life, but also to create a group of caregivers who will reach out to people in the congregation and the community whenever the need is perceived. Our society tries so hard to function as if there are no problems and no people in desperate need that a watchful eye and cocked ear are sometimes needed in order to find them. The pastor can be very helpful in this regard, but it is also the responsibility of the lay care group to look and listen for trouble as well; the pastor may sometimes be the *last* person to hear. The trained lay pastoral carers will be ready to be called upon by the minister, lay leader or other member of the group and will be able to respond to those who require help.

One task of the group is to survey the church and local community to note where it is necessary or beneficial to intervene. Nursing homes, schools for the handicapped, retirement complexes, and the like may be close to the church, but the voices of need are so muted that only an aggressive looking-and-listening will perceive them. There are likewise people within the church itself, crying out from loneliness, estrangement, or confusion, whose voices rarely reach beyond the walls of their own dwellings. The needs survey will help make group members sensitive to these pockets of distress.

In addition to the survey, it is also helpful to complete an assessment of readily available congregational resources (for example, the banker who can help people in financial crises, the person who will drive a cancer patient to the clinic, the piano student who will play for a music-loving shut-in, etc.).

Finally, monthly meetings of caregivers following the completion of formal training are highly recommended. These regular sessions serve several purposes. They provide for mutual support: pastoral care can be very gratifying and disappointing, exciting and frustrating, and mutual nourishment and consolation is of great benefit. The meetings also can be times when members continue reminding each other that what they are doing is a part of their own ministry in the Christian community. It is a response to "follow me," a way to love one's neighbor. The "failures"—when their attempts to reach out to others in Christian love are not received—can be reminders of the finitude and humanity of each person.

Monthly meetings also serve as opportunities for determining whether certain needs or people in need are being overlooked or for mutual consultation regarding people the caregivers are seeing. Their ministry is not offered in isolation. If one volunteer is "missing something" in visits with a particular nursing home resident, another lay person or the pastor can offer suggestions. If the group is large it is best to break into cells of five to six people who share with each other their experiences of caring during the month and seek suggestions for additional ways to help the people they are visiting.

Finally, the monthly meetings can provide a time for additional training beyond the basic work and an opportunity to apprise group members of further training opportunities available in the community. (These advanced training issues will be discussed in greater detail in the final chapter.)

Undertaking a lay pastoral care program within a congregation requires commitment to the task and to the changes it will produce, careful preparation, and thorough planning that covers not only the training but also the structure and functioning of the lay pastoral care group once it is begun. It is not a program that church leadership can launch and then expect to float on its own. It requires ongoing nurturing by *both* lay leaders and pastors. The task is an extensive (and extended) one—but the return is a greatly enhanced ministry, both in breadth and in quality, among the members of the congregation and to the community.

4

What Is
Lay Pastoral Care?

SESSION 1

- ☐ Breaking the ice—a "starter" to help people get to know each other and feel comfortable in the group (5–15 minutes)[1]
- ☐ Interpretation of what constitutes lay pastoral care (20–30 minutes)
- ☐ Description of the eight-week training course (10 minutes)
- ☐ Exercise on affirming your own gifts (25 minutes)
- ☐ Case discussion (30–45 minutes)
- ☐ Introduction of the ABC method of crisis intervention (15 minutes)

HOMEWORK[2]

1. Continue a review of Scripture selections. If time allows read chapter 2 of *The Caring Church* on the theology of lay pastoral care.
2. Look for and affirm gifts you already possess for pastoral care ministry with the expectation of sharing recent ways you have used them with the class during the next sessions.
3. Read chapter 5 of *The Caring Church*.

Of the eleven trainees who arrived at Emmanuel Church's first lay pastoral care session, most of them early, two groups knew each other well (four people from the early service and three from the eleven o'clock). They immediately sat together, in clusters. Except for two women who were in the same car pool, the remaining members knew the others by face only. The mood of the class was one of anticipation, mixed with nervousness and more than a few doubts, as they waited for the session to begin.

Breaking the Ice

It is extremely helpful for a group of people who are not altogether familiar with each other—such as the one at Emmanuel—to begin with an icebreaker. I loathe most "sensitivity games" and have found that when I use them they tend to make nervous people *more* nervous rather than less. Nevertheless, the class needs to begin with a low-threat way of getting acquainted. Each leader can find a method the group might be comfortable with; I have used several.

One icebreaker is to ask the participants to tell a little about themselves (including their avocations) and note their hopes and apprehensions concerning lay pastoral care ministry. A variation is to have them talk with each other in twos, then introduce their partners to the total group.

Another method that has been helpful for some groups is actually part of the second task of session 1 (interpretation). Groups of four to six people are formed to discuss Scripture passages or selections from theologians' writings that relate to pastoral care. Members of each group then report the group's understanding of the readings to the total group. The leader comments on the feedback and correlates it to the overall task of lay pastoral care. The use of Scripture in pastoral care visits will be treated in chapter 9.

Interpretation

A surprisingly large number of people who decide to join a class do not draw a direct relationship between helping others and Christ's dictum to "love your neighbor." They think pastoral care is something the *pastor* does—not something that *they* do. One of the leader's tasks is to communicate how the care that lay persons offer is as legitimate and efficacious as that which ordained clergy can give.

Pastoral care, of course, is to be distinguished from pastoral counseling. Pastoral care is the broader ministry, incorporating healing, sustaining, guiding, and reconciling; pastoral counseling is a more specialized task usually performed only by the pastor, who has specialized skills and training.

The task of interpretation can involve discussing such topics as how lay pastoral care has functioned historically within the tradition of the church; exploring Scripture to better understand love of neighbor; citing the theology of pastoral care by lay persons and especially the priesthood of all believers; noting that class members are already performing lay pastoral care and may not have recognized it; suggesting hindrances and helps for starting a lay ministry of pastoral care in one's church; and so on.

Any and all of the above can be a part of the interpretation stage of the first session. As the participants discover that pastoral care is not something the pastor offers alone but which every Christian performs, they will recognize that part of Jesus' call to "follow me" and "love one another" (or as Paul wrote, "bear one another's burdens") becomes a caring ministry to families, friends, neighbors, colleagues, members of the congregation, and many others.

It was noted above that one of the more beneficial ways of helping people get acquainted and assisting them in the theological interpretation of pastoral care is to discuss selections of Scripture or short theological readings.[3] The task of the small groups (four to six members each) is to explore together the selections' meanings as they relate to lay ministry and later to share the major themes with the whole class. The leader's role is to tie in these scriptural themes to a theology of lay ministry as well as to the tradition of the church as a whole and especially the parish's own denomination. See chapter 2 for further discussion of the theology of lay pastoral care. It is to be stressed that a part of the ministry or priesthood of all Christians—lay and clergy alike—is offering pastoral care to those whom we encounter in our daily lives.

Chapter 1 briefly listed some of the beliefs and attitudes on the part of both laity and clergy that may cause problems in the establishment of a lay pastoral care training program. During this first session, while interpreting what constitutes lay pastoral care, it is sometimes useful to discuss these and other hindrances with the class members. At the very least, the leader must be alert to inhibiting attitudes and confront them if they are encountered.

As already mentioned, the leader will have to watch for the belief that pastoral care is somehow synonymous with psychotherapy or counseling—which of course can only be offered by professionals.

It is good to explore specific ways in which class members already have given a ministry of care and then let the group suggest other possibilities. Some examples are: visiting a neighbor in the hospital after an accident; offering to drive a shut-in to church (a great opportunity for conversation); sharing a few moments of prayer with a friend waiting for biopsy results; bringing a casserole to a family whose child is in the hospital; stopping at the desk of a recently bereaved person for a friendly chat or an invitation to dinner; assisting the parents of a child who has run away; listening seriously to a neighbor, over a cup of coffee at the kitchen table, tell about the problems in her marriage; suggesting the name of a trusted pastor or counselor to a troubled adolescent; sharing your own experience of the liberation of the gospel to one overladen with guilt; and many others.

The knowledge that one has already been part of the pastoral care enterprise, without perhaps knowing what to call it, is especially helpful in quieting anxieties about one's capabilities for ministry. It also broadens the vision of what pastoral care is: not just counseling, not just something said. The Word mediates through actions as well as through spoken phrases.

Another possible hindrance is the trainees' apprehension that parishioners in need of help or care will hesitate to accept it from lay people. The fear is that people will say or think, "I only want to see the pastor," or, "I don't want to tell you [lay carer] anything because I don't want you to know these things about me."

Of course those parishioners who believe pastoral care can only be done by an ordained minister will be suspicious of others. It is therefore useful to communicate not only to the class but to the congregation as a whole that lay pastoral care already is happening in the congregation. If class members begin by visiting shut-ins and nursing home residents, people can be eased into the idea of pastoral care by the laity. (Congregations do not necessarily react negatively, however; in many churches lay pastoral care has taken place informally for decades, and the training will be viewed as a honing and improving of existing skills.) If hindrances exist, it is important that they be dealt with as part of the interpretation of what lay pastoral care is and how it functions.

Course Description

Following interpretation, it is helpful to devote a few minutes to describing how the course will be taught. Items to be explained are: homework and practice assignments (if any); attendance; shut-in or nursing home visitation requirements; and so on. Most of these items are covered in detail in chapter 3.

Allowing opportunity for questions along the way gives class members a chance to raise their own concerns about one component of the course or another. (The most common questions I have encountered deal with apprehensions about the "live" visitations that are to be assigned. A thorough explanation of the course during recruitment usually forestalls most fears and reservations.)

Affirming Your Own Gifts

An exercise that will aid the interpretation task, while highlighting the fact that lay pastoral care is not some totally new or different method of relating to others, is "affirming your own gifts." The leader reads 1 Corinthians 12:1-11 and makes the point that each Christian has been given a unique set of gifts unlike anyone else's. (See appendix B for a handout that can be used at this point.)

The class members are then asked to write five of their own strengths or gifts that will benefit their caring for others, being very specific. Several examples can be given to stimulate their thinking, such as: "I am good at listening"; "I work as a nurse, and so I'm comfortable with visiting people in the hospital"; "I'm a handyman and can do small fix-ups at a shut-in's house"; "I give people the benefit of the doubt and don't jump on their case immediately"; "I'm willing to try anything"; "My husband died five years ago and I know what it's like to lose someone you love"; "I am very patient."

After members have listed five strengths, they share their lists in pairs or small groups of four to six persons and give examples of these strengths to each other. Such sharing usually generates considerable conversation in the groups. After five or ten minutes the leader asks members to contribute items from their lists to the total group, frequently responding to their suggestions by asking, "Would you give an example of that?" Gifts are recorded on a chalkboard.

After each gift is listed, the leader can mention how that particular gift could be used in pastoral care (some are obvious; others may be more obscure). Almost any item that is introduced can be related in some way to caregiving—though the leader may have to emphasize a different aspect of the gift. For example, "I'm good at giving advice" may bring the leader's response: "Yes, and the ability to listen is not always sufficient. It is frequently necessary for people to look at their alternatives and make a decision. Sometimes they don't know where they can get help, and some advice about referral agencies or where the jobs are, for example, can be invaluable."

This "affirming your own gifts" exercise will continue the interpretation task and help members see that they are already offering pastoral care and can grow in their ability to give such care in the future.

Case Studies

One change I have made in training lay pastoral carers since this book was first released is the introduction of case discussions— which usually is the most compelling part of the first class session. Participants are better able to see how they can minister to others and how to use their own unique gifts through this exercise than through the other teaching methods used.

At the completion of the section on "affirming your own gifts," the class again breaks into the same small groups of four-six people and discusses one of the cases found in appendix C. The leader assigns a different case to every group. (Cases other than those found in appendix C that better reflect the typical situations found in each local church may be developed.) Groups answer two basic questions concerning the case: (1) What is happening to this person or family? What is your assessment of the situation? (2) What pastoral care can be offered by group members? What help can be offered by other members of the church? How would you go about initiating the lay pastoral care?

After small group discussion, each group reports to the total class how they would handle the situation. This gives the full class a chance to consider all the cases and allows the leader to further define lay pastoral care and theologically interpret the care offered.

It also helps people to see, at this early stage in their training, that they can do something of significance.

The final task of the first session is to introduce the topic of the second class meeting and, if time allows, the rudiments of a method for giving care in times of crisis.

The ABC Method of Crisis Intervention

Not all pastoral care addresses crisis situations. However, crises are particularly stressful times for people, and the ABC method of crisis intervention is an effective model to follow in these cases. Presented here is my adaptation of a procedure first outlined by Warren L. Jones and later revised by a number of theorists.[4] It is important to note that the method does not necessarily progress from A to B to C—and in fact the steps usually overlap—but it can be used as a general guideline for offering care. Its genius is that the basic procedure is easy to remember, even in the midst of upsetting situations, by people who have no counseling background.

A: *Achieving contact,* or establishing a relationship, relaxes the person in distress and makes effective communication possible. Trust, warmth, and empathy are as important in lay pastoral care during a crisis as in any other form of care. Fortunately, since persons in crisis tend to be less defensive than at other times in their lives, this step often requires less time and effort than it would in other situations. Achieving contact amounts to establishing a relationship, using listening and attending skills that will be covered in session 2.

B: *Boiling down* the problem to its essentials requires defining what has happened, what is being felt, and why. The helper will have fewer and shorter periods of mere listening and will focus on the present situation and source of the stress or threat, weed out irrelevant data, and respond to the crucial nonverbal behaviors, feelings, and meanings. In boiling down the problem, it is particularly important to recognize both the feeling and the content behind the feeling (which together equal the meaning) and if possible mutually arrive at a verbal expression of this understanding with the individual. Boiling down especially involves the responding skills to be discussed in session 3.

C: *Coping actively* with the problem is the final step, in which the individual is helped to assemble resources, plan an attack on the problem, and actually make changes designed to resolve the situation. The person looks at the various courses of action that are available and acts upon one or more of them. The C of the ABC method can involve referral of the troubled individual to someone who is able to offer the particular type of assistance needed.

The skills of guiding a person to cope actively with a problem are discussed at length in session 7. The lay pastoral carer can help the individual establish goals in terms that are as specific as possible; take inventory of resources both internal and external that can provide strength, support, and assistance; develop a catalogue of possible options for achieving the goals; take action; and finally, review and refine those goals and actions.

In the first, introductory session of lay pastoral care training, ideas are presented concerning the nature and function of pastoral care and the scope of the laity's traditional ministry of care to the lonely, troubled, and needy world. Class members are made aware of the many skills and gifts they already bring to the task. They also are introduced to a system of responding to people in need that breaks the process into easily remembered steps and can lend clarity and direction (even in the week immediately ahead) to all their loving acts.

5

The Care Relationship

SESSION 2
- ☐ Review of the ABC method (10 minutes)
- ☐ Discussion on establishing a relationship (20 minutes)
- ☐ Listing and practice of attending behaviors (45 minutes)
- ☐ Explanation and role play of listening skills (45 minutes)

HOMEWORK
1. Practice attending and listening skills with several close acquaintances or relatives.
2. Read chapter 6 of *The Caring Church.*

Relationships are important! Most of us know from personal experience what it is like to be temporarily without close friendships. A move to another part of the country, an upsetting loss through divorce or death—all point out the hunger we have for relatedness.

Review

At the beginning of session 2, devoted to the skills of establishing relationships, the leader will want to briefly review the ABC method presented at the close of session 1, especially since it is essentially an introduction to a process of caregiving that begins with a relationship of love and trust.

Establishing a Relationship

The A of the ABC method just reviewed requires the carer to achieve a workable relationship with the person in need. Establishing this relationship is a troubling aspect of lay pastoral care for many trainees. "I don't know what to say" is the way their concern is generally expressed. It is important to recognize that lay care relationships are formed in a similar manner to other kinds of relationships. There is nothing magical or mystical in what the pastor does in this regard; indeed, almost all relationships are initiated by *attending* physically to the person and *listening* carefully to what is said. This would be true if you were selling insurance, getting to know a new neighbor, courting a future spouse, teaching a class, counseling an alcoholic, or inviting a new member of the community to your church. The relationship established is the foundation upon which the decision is based to buy the insurance, continue to grow in friendship with the neighbor, marry, take another course from the teacher, consider giving up drinking, or join the church. The relationship is obviously not the only reason why such decisions are made—but it is a key element in all of them.

Relationships can be for good or ill. Think of the times you have been disgruntled with the way a person acted in a relationship. You commented to another, "I'd never go to that church, the pastor is so cold!" or, "I'd never buy a thing from him—all he was interested in was making a sale," or of a doctor, "She had no bedside manner. She was in and out of my room in less than two minutes."

A number of psychotherapists have noted that an effectively functioning therapist-client relationship is the critical contributor to positive outcome of the counseling process.[1] In other words, a tender, warm, realistic, and empathetic relationship can help the counselee develop understandings and make changes necessary for the resolution of a problem. On the other hand, a relationship characterized by fear, mistrust, coldness, insensitivity, and domination by one person will most likely lead to little or no positive change.

Goldstein has pointed out that "many people obtain similar benefits as a result of their interactions with a wide variety of other types of helpers [than a psychotherapist]—friends, clergymen, bartenders, relatives, counselors, nurses, and so forth. . . . Perhaps, many . . . researchers have proposed, some of the causes of such changes can be identified by determining what ingredients successful psychotherapy and successful help from others have in common."[2] As noted above, one of those common ingredients— if not the key ingredient—is a good relationship.

In short, the relationship is the foundation upon which all pastoral care is built and is the base of all care offered. Relationships are developed in essentially the same manner whether they are for business, personal, or helping purposes. We tend to feel good and trusting in a relationship, or uneasy and mistrustful. The more comfortable, at ease, and trustful a relationship is, the more willing we are to hear what the other has to say—especially when what is said confronts us with what we do not wish to examine. Not only is a relationship the foundation for all care offered: a good relationship is frequently the key to whether change will occur and positive resolution will be achieved through the help offered.

Finally, the pastoral care relationship is the vessel—fragile and imperfect though it may be—through which the Word of God can address the other person. A solid, caring relationship can allow the Word a better chance of being heard than one poorly developed and characterized by feelings of upset over the other's failings. I do not intend to encapsulate or limit the Word of God; it moves when and where it will, in the least as well as the most ideal circumstances. But I would compare the Word to a seed that may sprout and even grow in parched and rocky soil, but is far more likely to flourish if it falls in a bed that has been carefully prepared, watered, and fed—like a carefully cultivated, good, caring relationship.

What are the component skills for establishing a successful pastoral care relationship? Four will be discussed herein: (1) attending behaviors; (2) listening skills; (3) responding skills; and (4) problem solving, decision, and action. The first two, attending and listening, are vital in the initiation of a relationship.

Attending Behaviors

Attending behaviors are the physical, nonverbal ways in which a helper says, "I care," to the person in difficulty. They are important parts of achieving a relationship with the individual.

Some valuable attending behaviors include symbolic nourishing, posture, touching, eye contact, and a conducive physical environment.

Symbolic Nourishing

Probably the earliest attending behavior in your experience was the nourishing you received at your mother's breast. For the rest of your life, one of the simplest and most effective ways in which you perceive the concern and caring of others is through the offering of some kind of food or drink and thus, symbolically, emotional nourishment as well. Bringing a salad or casserole to a bereaved family, taking an employee out to lunch to discuss problems on the job, baking a coffee cake for a friend who is going through a divorce, offering a cup of coffee or even a glass of water to a person who is telling you about a painful experience—these are a few ways of symbolically feeding people in need.

Posture

Often referred to as "body language," the way you sit and move communicates your interest or lack of interest in what is going on around you. If you slouch back in your chair, fidget, look at your watch repeatedly, or fall asleep (it has happened!), the person who is talking will receive the clear message that you would rather be almost anywhere else. On the other hand, if you face the individual, lean forward slightly, and remain calm but attentive, you will communicate your interest in what she or he is saying and feeling. Remember also that as much caring is done while standing leaning against a coke machine in a hospital cafeteria or walking a country lane as is done just sitting.

Touching

Going back again to the time of infancy, being held and cuddled is another very basic way in which you experienced love from parents and others. The need for "stroking" continues into adulthood. Holding the hand of a person in grief, putting your arm around the shoulder of one who is upset, even a handshake, are ways of gently communicating your concern through touch without threatening the individual. All attending behaviors, but especially touching, must be offered only if they will be of assistance to the person. (Be aware that in care relationships with people of the opposite sex, touching may be interpreted as a sexual gesture.) The great benefit of touch is that it may transmit feelings of concern when words are impossible.

Eye Contact

If you have ever tried to carry on a conversation with someone who wouldn't look you in the eyes, you know how important eye contact can be for two-way communication. The amount of need for eye contact varies considerably from one person to the next. I first learned about this one day in college. While I was getting further clarification on a point after that day's lecture, the professor turned from me and began erasing the blackboard. Without realizing it, I stopped talking. He turned back toward me and said, "You need eye contact." I replied, "Huh?" He went on to explain that I and many other individuals are not able to carry on a conversation without looking into the other's eyes. Most people (like me, at the time) do not even know they have such a need, and without sufficient eye contact will tend to share their problems more slowly and superficially; they may even stop talking whenever you look away!

Environment

It is important whenever possible to provide an environment that is comfortable and relaxed and communicates stability, openness, and confidentiality. Ideally you should both be sitting in comfortable chairs of equal height, facing each other. Doors to the room should be shut and noises from the outside not allowed to intrude, so the person has confidence that he or she cannot be overheard. If the room is reasonably orderly, not chaotic, and the temperature and lighting at comfortable levels, the individual will be more relaxed.

It is of course understood that care may be offered in a kitchen, walking city streets, standing in an emergency ward, or leaning against a light pole; the environment cannot always be ideal. Nevertheless, every possible attempt should be made to talk in a place that is relaxed and conducive to private conversation. Therefore, you may move from the living room to the privacy of the den; leave the group at the street corner and find a quiet coffee shop; take the individual out of the hospital waiting room for a few moments of respite in the chapel. The setting where listening occurs can greatly affect the openness of the troubled person to your attempts at caring.

A simple and yet very effective way for class members to grasp the full import of attending behaviors on the establishment of a relationship is to practice both good and bad attending behaviors. In this exercise dyads are formed, made up of talkers and listeners. The talkers share a recent, moderately troubling situation they have encountered personally. They are to continue talking (no matter what else the leader says) until the leader says, "Stop." The listeners, meanwhile, practice all of the previously mentioned attending behaviors, listening and saying nothing more than "uh-huh" until the leader calls, "Switch." At that moment, they are to begin breaking all the rules of attending behavior—looking away, slouching in their chairs, yawning, and so on. When the exercise is completed roles are reversed and it is repeated. Subsequently the leader can ask the groups, "What was it like when your listener stopped attending?" The discussion that ensues is usually quite lively!

Listening

Another important way to communicate caring and concern is through the way you hear what the other person is saying. To quote Dietrich Bonhoeffer:

> The first service that one owes to others in the fellowship consists in listening to them. Just as love of God begins with listening to His Word, so the beginning of love for the brethren is learning to listen to them. It is God's love for us that He not only gives us His Word but also lends us His ear. So it is His work that we do for our brother when we learn to listen to him. Christians, especially ministers, so often think they must always contribute something when they are in the company of others, that this is the one service they have to render. They forget that listening can be a greater service than speaking.[3]

Bonhoeffer has rightly captured an important stance of the Christian: to listen, whether to God or neighbor. It may be the key skill of lay pastoral carers as they offer themselves to others.

The following are suggestions for effective listening. (After a review of the suggestions listed below, the remaining time—if any—is given to the practice of listening. A role play or any of the responding exercises in Chapter 6 can be used to close the session. Participants will need time to debrief mutually any exercises they complete.)

Allow no distractions—no phone calls, noises, daydreaming or worrying, interruptions, or anything else. Be careful not to lose yourself in your own thoughts or concerns, which will naturally hinder you from hearing what the other has to say. People have a way of knowing when you are distracted.

Make sure your attending behaviors are appropriate to what is being said—you may laugh with those who are laughing or cry with a person in tears. When your attending behaviors are not congruent with the feelings being expressed, it will be more difficult for you to listen effectively, as well as for the other to talk freely.

Know what you are listening for—the cause behind the problem, what the person is feeling, what methods already have been tried to resolve the problem, and so forth.

Temporarily suspend all judgment, especially early in the relationship, and allow the person to release pent-up emotions. If you immediately begin criticizing, he or she will be reticent to continue sharing. Judgment as a part of pastoral care may sometimes be called for—but not until a solid relationship is established.

Be patient. There may be long pauses while the disturbed and often confused individual sorts out feelings and events and tries to talk about things that are almost impossible to verbalize. Most beginning trainees are overly anxious about filling in these silences; therefore, instead of listening, they try to figure out what they are going to say next. But when people are upset words do not come easily, and halting speech and long silences are to be expected. Filling those pauses actually hinders the troubled from accurately saying what needs to be expressed.

Listen for important themes being reiterated by the individual. Especially crucial themes can be recognized because they will be either stated with great intensity or repeatedly brought up in the conversation. (Good sermons do the same thing; important points are made with an especially strong "oomph" or are reiterated in different ways to let the listener know of their significance.) The lay pastoral carer listens intently for these important themes since they will be valuable in helping persons look at the essence of their distress.

While establishing the relationship, communicate as much as possible your own self-confidence, stability, intensity, and willingness to take an active role. Particularly in a crisis, a troubled individual may initially be unable to act or decide to take any responsibility alone and needs to sense this strength within the pastoral carer. The way you *attend* and *listen* will communicate the genuineness of your love and the depth of your involvement.

6
Listening and Responding

SESSION 3

☐ Reflections on last week's homework (practicing attending and listening) and review of what constitutes a lay pastoral care relationship (15–30 minutes)

☐ Demonstration of nonfacilitative ways of relating (15–20 minutes)

☐ Discussion and demonstration of facilitative responding—mirroring

☐ Practice of facilitative responding (this and the preceding item together: 60–90 minutes)

HOMEWORK

1. Practice mirroring with several people during the course of the week.
2. Read chapter 7 of *The Caring Church*.

"It was really fantastic. I couldn't believe it," exclaimed one young woman when her leader asked, "How did your attending and listening homework go?" She continued, "One afternoon my seven-year-old came in crying. He had been in a fight with a neighborhood boy—he'd been in a number of fights with this boy. Instead of telling him he shouldn't fight, as I usually do, I stopped and listened to him. I think this is probably the first time I've really spent more than a minute listening to anything he had to say. He began to pour out a tale of woe about this bully picking on him and how he tried to avoid a fight. All this time I had assumed he was really

59

starting it. But now I am convinced he's trying to stay out of the fights and is having difficulty doing it."

Reflections and Review

Such enthusiastic reports of the previous week's homework assignment, to practice attending and listening with close friends and family, will be common among the lay pastoral care trainees. In the same session mentioned above, a grocery store manager responded to the leader's questions:

"I usually keep on doing what I'm doing when someone comes up to talk to me. I'm so busy, and there is so much work to keeping the store going, that I can't stop every time someone has a question or a problem. But after last Thursday's meeting, I decided I hadn't been fair to some of the employees and thought I would give them a fairer shake. So several times this week when someone came up with a problem, instead of just snapping back at them I stopped for a few minutes and listened to the problem and tried to be as understanding as I could. I wasn't always that understanding, but I was impressed how people seemed to feel better talking about it even when there wasn't a solution. One woman wanted a weekend off to go on a short trip with some friends. Instead of just saying no, I listened to her tell about the trip, and how excited she was about it, and how exhausted she felt and her need to get away. I told her I really wanted her working that weekend, but if she could get someone else to cover for the full weekend, then I would agree to do it."

Another woman in the class decided to try attending to and listening to her husband's mother, age sixty-nine, who lived with them. She told the group, "I tend to tune her out all the time because all she ever does is criticize this or criticize that, criticize how I handle the kids, criticize someone in the church, criticize my cooking, or complain about how no one ever comes to visit her. I get so tired of listening to it that I really don't even hear her any more. After class I decided to try to do my homework assignment and listen to what she was saying. I tried to take your suggestion and listen to the pain that she had. She started up as usual complaining and criticizing, but I think she realized after a while that I was really listening to her this time, and she began to cry and tell me how useless she felt. She actually cried for quite a while. I didn't realize how bad she was feeling or how lonely she was, but I don't know what to do now. I mean, she's back to complaining again, and I don't know if I can take off and give her that much attention every time she wants to talk. What can I do?"

After further discussion from different class members, the leader noted, "I know that listening and using the attending behaviors didn't work like magic for everyone. What about some of the problems you had?" After a period of uncomfortable silence, one man asked the question, "How long should you listen before you ask a question?" The leader replied, "Why don't you tell me how the homework assignment went for you?" After some talk it was apparent that the man believed listening was something you had to endure until you could start asking questions and telling people what to do. Several others had similar questions. The conversation about the homework assignment led the leader to review what constitutes the skills of developing a care relationship, and also to discuss some nonfacilitative methods of responding, listed below.

Nonfacilitative Ways of Responding

If class members are to know how to go beyond attending and listening and begin boiling the problem down to its essentials, it is necessary for them to understand facilitative and nonfacilitative ways of responding. Perhaps the best way of doing this is through a demonstration of both.

The leader, using a class volunteer, may play the role of pastoral carer and demonstrate some or all of the following unhelpful responses. These demonstrations need not be longer than a minute or two—just enough time for class members to visualize the scene.

Advice Giving

One of the quickest ways to miss the pain of others and leave them feeling unheard is to offer quick advice. For example, giving advice only ten minutes after a person starts talking does not take seriously what the other has to say or the complexity of the issues involved. Furthermore, the advice probably will not be followed because it is given before a solid relationship has been established. The tentative offering of advice can be helpful, but only after a caring relationship has been founded and alternative strategies of action have been explored.

Reassurance

Telling a wife whose husband has just left her, "I'm sure he'll come back," or a person going into exploratory surgery, "Everything is going to be just fine," is not helpful. Such statements are based on knowledge you do not possess. Most people reject such reassurances as insincere—they may even mumble inaudibly, "How do *you* know?" It is desirable to support an individual emotionally and to be realistically reassuring; it is inauthentic and inappropriate to promise what is impossible to predict.

Platitudes

Complex problems are sometimes summarized by well-meaning but ineffectual helpers in the form of platitudes. "God helps those who help themselves"; "If you make your bed, you have to lie in it"; "A fellow ought to go out and sow some wild oats before he settles down"—all contain some kernels of truth but are not very personal. Responses ought to be specific, clear, and individually tailored to the issues the troubled person is talking about. The greater the specificity of a response, the greater the applicability of the help offered.

Closed-Ended Questions

"How old are you?" "Did you want to marry him in the first place?" "How many years did you go together?" "Did you love her?" Such questions only call for a word or a phrase in reply and do not allow people to tell their own stories, *in their own ways.* The number of questions you ask should be kept to a minimum; questions tend to put people on the spot and narrow the range within which they can tell you of their pain. When queries are called for they need to be open ended: "Recently, how have you felt about your husband?" "What are your concerns about this operation?" "What is it like at home now that your last daughter has moved out?" "Tell me about. . . ."

Evaluative Statements

Pronouncements such as "That's dumb," "You were foolish to tell your husband about your affair," or "A Christian should not smoke," are apt to do more harm than good. Although God's love is meted out in both judgment and grace and it is difficult for Christians to remain morally neutral, passing judgment—especially early in a relationship—does not take seriously the complexities of the person's problems. After a relationship is well established and considerable listening has occurred, it may be appropriate to give witness to your understanding of the ethics of a particular situation. When doing this, be very tentative and gentle, allowing the person to see your compassion and hear the concern that leads you to say what you do. A word of judgment is best stated not in anger but out of kindness for the other. Be especially careful not to *blame* the individual.

Interpretations

Sometimes, in an effort to be good pastoral carers, lay persons will mimic what they believe a psychiatrist or psychologist would do in the situation and make interpretations. Statements like "That's probably because of the harsh treatment your mother gave you" or "You're doing that because you don't like women" are examples of interpretive responses that are not helpful. Leave psychoanalysis to therapists' offices and cocktail parties, and respond directly to what has been said. Let each individual draw her or his *own* conclusions.

Arguing

Debating with a person who is experiencing difficulties usually creates distance rather than closeness. Respect the right of a person to hold views that are different from your own; avoid criticizing or belittling others because of your differences.

Inappropriate Sharing

It is very effective for you to share, as one finite human being with another, the struggles or joys you have experienced. But it is not appropriate for you to use the relationship as a place to seek your own help or release. Get that help, if you need it, from other lay carers or from the pastor.[1]

Facilitative Ways of Responding

Probably the best way to develop effective (facilitative) responding skills is to learn mirroring, or reflecting back in a sentence or two the essence of the feelings and content the other person is sharing.

It is sometimes difficult for class members to fully understand this, so after the leader discusses and demonstrates the mirroring of feelings the class may wish to do any or all of the following exercises. (Exercise 3 is the essential practice of mirroring; exercises 1 and 2, which should be done if time allows, introduce a developmental sequence of skills that enhance the ability to mirror.)

The first exercise is used to expand peoples' feeling vocabulary. The leader tells the class he or she is going to suggest a feeling word and they will have two minutes to write as many responses as they can to the phrase, "I hear you saying you feel _____." (They are to fill in the blank.) The trainees write all of the synonyms they can (words, phrases, or colloquialisms) for one of the following words suggested by the leader: happy, sad, angry, frustrated, and so on. If some class members are not able to come up with more than five or six words or phrases, it is suggested that they practice at home writing down at least fifty words or phrases for each of the above feelings and any others that are thought to be helpful.

In exercise 2, another exercise designed to hone the trainees' responding skills, the leader plays the role of "client" in a thirty-second to two-minute portion of a care situation and asks class members to write a word or phrase that fills in the blank: "I hear you saying you feel _____." Group members report their replies out loud. The leader then indicates how accurately they have reflected the feelings of the person in the role play ("not very close," "close," "very close," "that's it exactly," etc.). If individuals miss the mark, they should know that what they said may have been right for someone else, but not for the particular individual in the role. Some typical care situations for the exercise are the following:

a. a twenty-three-year-old housewife, married four years, whose husband has just left her;
b. a forty-three-year-old father who is angry at his seventeen-year-old daughter because of her low grades;
c. a twenty-one-year-old college student near the end of his schooling who is uncertain about what career to enter;
d. a grieving husband whose wife of thirty-four years has recently died;
e. a graduating college senior who has just been accepted as a teacher in the school system she wanted to work for;

f. the parents of a twenty-seven-year-old son who has just been diagnosed with AIDS;

g. a very depressed fifty-seven-year-old woman who has no one in the world to whom she feels close [do not say a word in this situation; use only nonverbal gestures].

In the third exercise, which specifically concentrates on mirroring, the class separates into dyads with a speaker and a responder. The person who talks shares a recent, moderately troubling personal event. Every minute or so, the responder practices mirroring by retelling in a sentence or two the basic meaning of what the speaker has said. After ten minutes of this exercise the two discuss how accurately the responder picked up on the talker's feelings. They subsequently switch roles and repeat the exercise. The leader floats around the room, spending time with any dyads that are having difficulties with the task.

Trainees need to become aware that, although in establishing a relationship it is best to respond primarily to feelings at first, as the relationship develops both feelings and content are increasingly important since the two together reveal the *meaning* of what is being expressed. For example: "I hear you saying you feel low" reflects a feeling (depression), whereas "because you lost your job" reflects content (being fired). Only when the two are viewed together is the full meaning apparent. We understand why the depression is there when we add the content—the loss of a job. The third exercise can be repeated during this and future sessions, with the responder reflecting *both* feelings and content.

The above exercises, or others the leader creates, may be used to assist in developing responding skills. Practice is important, and the homework assignment is vital. Participants will almost always enhance their ability to establish relationships if they practice mirroring during the following week.

Finally, either during the discussion of mirroring or as a closing to the session, the leader can share the following hints about effective responding or giving good feedback to another.

Be specific. Vague or general responses such as, "You are too aggressive," are hard for the person to use.

Use open-ended questions. Ask as few questions as possible and make them open-ended, requiring more than a simple yes or no.

Describe rather than evaluate. It is more desirable to describe how you feel about something the person has said than to put a label on it.

Respond with immediacy. It is important to give frequent feedback at the appropriate time rather than to save it all up for a long summarization.

Be brief. Try to keep most responses down to a sentence or two whenever possible.

Check to see that you understand correctly. If you are at all uncertain whether you have rightly interpreted what one has said—or whether you have been misunderstood—check to see that the two of you are on the same wavelength. One way is to have the other rephrase what he or she heard you saying (that is, mirror back to you).

Pause. It is best to allow lapses in conversation whenever they occur naturally. It is a very common mistake to pepper the dialogue with new questions whenever the person takes a breath. Pauses not only allow the individual to reflect on what has been said but also give the lay carer opportunity to formulate responses without using valuable "listening time" to do so.

The demonstrations, enactments, and exercises of the third session are designed to engage trainees in a very active learning-by-doing through which they can build the skills and confidence necessary for sensitively listening and responding to people in need of their care.

7

Hospital and Shut-In Visitation

Session 4

□ Discussion of shut-in, nursing home, and hospital visits (30–40 minutes)

□ Demonstration of a visit to a nursing home resident (20–25 minutes)

□ Role play between class members of a nursing home visit (60 minutes)

Homework

1. Visit two or three assigned individuals in a nearby nursing home. The task is to call on each person at least once in the following two weeks; during the sixth session class time will be devoted to questions and concerns that are raised by these visits. (If the leader wants for only one week to elapse between the assignment of visits and the discussion, this homework task can be delayed by one week.)

2. Read chapter 8 of *The Caring Church*.

Sally Lopez had already made several visits as a lay pastoral carer to residents of a local nursing home. She had not been in the hospital herself for many years but had made several trips to the emergency ward with one or another of her three children, and recently had visited her next-door neighbor after an emergency appendectomy. Even so, the prospect of doing the first hospital visit requested by the pastor left her uneasy.

Sally was not acquainted with Mrs. Tyler, the elderly woman she was to visit. She knew the woman was a member of her church but could not get out of the house to attend services. Five days earlier, Mrs. Tyler had fallen and had broken her hip. Walking down the hall, Sally noticed that characteristic hospital smell, and it made her feel even more uncomfortable. So did the sight of gurneys wheeling patients who were attached to tubes and bottles. She began to wonder why she had agreed to make the visit.

After checking with the ward nurse and knocking on Mrs. Tyler's door, Sally entered the room.

LAY PASTORAL CARER: Hello, Mrs. Tyler. I'm Sally Lopez from First Christian Church.

PATIENT: [*looking away from the TV in the room*]: Let me turn this thing off. [*She does.*] What did you say your name was?

LPC: I'm Sally Lopez from First Christian. The pastor said you had had an accident and might appreciate a visit.

P: Oh, yes, come in and sit down. You can use that chair over there [*pointing to the far wall*]; nobody is using it. [*Pause.*] Lopez— you're Christiana's daughter-in-law, aren't you?

LPC: Yes, I am.

P: Yes, I thought so. Back when I could get around I used to know your husband's mother. How is she, anyway?

LPC: Just fine. She had some problems with her neck a few months ago—it caused numbness in her hands—but it's better now.

P: That's good. [*She wiggles in bed to get comfortable.*] I'm glad.

LPC: How are you doing?

P: [*sighing*] Better. They have been giving me a lot of shots, and it seems all I do is sleep. Today is the first day I've been awake and felt much good.

The two women then conversed very naturally about how Mrs. Tyler felt, how she had feared she might die after her fall because no one had been at home and she had not been able to reach a phone, how her son-in-law had stopped over after work and had found her. Sally felt much more comfortable after talking with Mrs. Tyler. She had merely asked a few questions and Mrs. Tyler, who had few living friends able to visit her, did most of the talking. Sally had needed to do little more than offer a reflection or pose a question now and then.

Realizing she should not stay too long since Mrs. Tyler was most likely weak from the operation on her hip, Sally chose to bring the visit to an end even though Mrs. Tyler kept chatting enthusiastically.

LPC: Well, Mrs. Tyler, I've *really* enjoyed our visit, but I think I'd better leave so you can get your rest. [*She definitely means the "really," because it has been easier than she anticipated and she feels she has something to offer and is needed.*]

P: I appreciate your coming. I hope you can come again.

LPC: If you like. I'd be happy to. How long are you going to be here?

P: The doctors say I'll have to be here for a while yet—they won't give me a date.

LPC: I'll be back Friday or Saturday, then; is that okay?

P: That would be fine.

LPC: Before I go, is there anything I can do for you? Are there any reading materials you'd like? Some magazines? [*Pause*] Or can I bring you anything from your home?

P: No, nothing . . . maybe a couple of news magazines . . . no, my eyes are not very good, and I can't read like I used to.

LPC: Is there anything else?

P: Nothing I can think of. [*Pause*] You can pray for me and ask the pastor to.

LPC: Would you like to pray now? [*Sally's anxieties increase some with this question; she does not think she is very good at offering prayers.*]

P: That would be nice.

LPC: What would you like to share with Jesus?

P: Oh, thank him for guiding the hands of the doctors, and . . . [*pause*] for my daughter and son-in-law who I am a burden to at times . . . [*pause*] and that Jesus will be here.

LPC: Okay, let's pray. [*Both close their eyes and Sally grasps one of Mrs. Tyler's hands, which lies at the side of the bed.*] Dear God, thank you for this day. . . . And thank you for Mrs. Tyler. Thank you also for the many people who are caring for her here . . . the surgeons and doctors and nurses. Thank you also for her family. We ask you to be with all these people and especially with Mrs. Tyler as she mends from her fall and her operation. In Jesus' name, Amen.

Lay visitation in hospitals, nursing homes, or in the homes of shut-ins is one of the most significant forms of care that can be offered by lay people. The fourth session is totally devoted to this activity.

Discussion of Visitation

The session may begin with two members of the class reading a verbatim account of a pastoral visit, such as the one recounted above. If a couch is available, the "patient" may lie down and lend some realism to the scenario.

After the verbatim is read, class members are urged to ask questions, comment on how they might do it differently, and share any anxieties they have about this type of visitation. Some may have reservations about doing these visits, and the dramatization will help to surface their concerns.

When questioning and sharing begins to slow (or when time runs short) the leader can review each item discussed in the next section—Visiting the Sick or Shut-In—inviting questions and comments. It is especially effective if a member of the class—such as a nurse or a nursing home attendant—can help in the presentation of the suggestions.

Visiting the Sick or Shut-In

Don't stay too long, particularly on a hospital visit—make the period very short if the person is in critical condition or appears very tired. Frequently five or ten minutes is enough for someone who is acutely ill.

Rudolph E. Grantham comments, "How long you stay in a room is usually determined by your closeness to the patient, by his or her physical and emotional condition at the time, and by the purpose of your visit. To some patients, we are a necessary source of strength; to others, a good friend who wears like an old shoe; and to other patients, we are guests who must be entertained."[1] The lay pastoral carer must assess which of these he or she is to the patient, and judge the length of the visit accordingly. (It should be noted that visits to shut-ins and those in nursing homes usually can last longer than hospital calls.) Watch the patient's nonverbal behavior, especially facial expressions, for indications that it is time to leave.

Don't stay at all if the patient has family present and they appear to be involved in private conversation.

A good example of this was experienced by my wife recently when she traveled 2500 miles to be with her father who was having cancer surgery. She had not seen her parents for three years, her sister for five, and other family members for even longer. Yet during the course of the day no less than four pastors and several lay persons came, stayed, visited, prayed, and were generally intrusive in what needed to be a time for the family to reestablish some closeness and minister to each other. Know when to say a few words of greeting and concern, and then leave.

Be aware that patients will sometimes act in aberrant ways, not only because of shock or the effects of illness, but because of medications they are taking.

Sit in a place where you can be seen easily. If the person is not able to roll over or sit up, remain standing so she or he can look at you without tiring (don't stand in the path of sunlight or other bright light, however). Suggest to the hospital patient that you pull a curtain between the two of you and the next bed, to offer more privacy. No smoking, of course!

Suggest a change of scene. In a hospital or nursing home, suggest to an ambulatory patient that the two of you go to a waiting room, lounge, cafeteria, chaplain's room, or some other place. If it is not possible to leave the hospital room, be aware of the needs of any other patients in the room who could be very sick or in great pain.

It is best to visit a hospital patient during visiting hours. Likewise, in a nursing home or even private residence, find out what times would be ideal for visiting (avoid nap times and meal times). When you have arrived outside the room, check with the ward nurse or attendant to see if the patient is receiving visitors; some people do not want to see anyone when they are ill. Knock on the door before you enter. If medical personnel arrive to perform certain procedures, excuse yourself and return when they have finished. If the person is asleep, leave a note and return at another time.

If you wish to offer help, be specific; for example, to a young mother in the hospital, "Would you like me to drive your daughter to school?" or to a shut-in who has twisted her ankle, "I'd like to bring in supper tomorrow evening, is that okay?" A general offer—"What can I do to help?" calls for more creativity and assertiveness than most patients can muster, and is likely to receive a "Nothing, thanks very much" response.

The care you give is not just for the person in the bed, but also for the relatives and close friends of the sick. Part of your time may be spent with them. But do remember that the last sense people lose is their sense of hearing, and be careful when talking in a quiet voice to nurses or relatives. Hushed conversation can indicate to the sick individual—even one who appears to be co-matose—that things are worse than they seem, or even that death may be around the corner. When speaking to the patient, adjust your voice level to the individual's hearing—especially if he or she wears a hearing aid. It is helpful occasionally to ask if you are speaking too softly (or too loudly).

Use physical gestures to express your caring—touching, patting, stroking, and so forth.

When praying, listen to the patient's requests. Do not assume you know what they are. Ask, "What concerns would you like to bring to the Lord?" and invite the person to join you in prayer.

Encourage hope without giving false assurances. Grantham says, "Be cheerful, but don't force cheerfulness if you don't feel it. . . . One good rule is to enter the room with a neutral mood tone—no excessive joy or sympathy. It is better for you to adjust to the patient's mood than for him or her to adjust to yours."[2]

Listen carefully to what is concerning or upsetting the person, and do not make assumptions about what might be the problem.

Try to help the person relax and use your time effectively. Many sick people may not know how to act during your visit—especially those who are not close to the church—so be sensitive to this possibility. Your presence could even spell impending doom . . . a sign that things are worse than they seem.

Prepare yourself to work with the sick, especially in hospitals or nursing homes. If you find the institutional atmosphere difficult to handle, you would do well to desensitize yourself to it (for example, tour a local hospital with a member of the congregation who is a nurse or visit a friend who works in a home for the mentally retarded, in each case approaching the visits in a relaxed manner, spending time, asking questions, and making repeated calls until the surroundings are more comfortable to you). You also need to realize that visiting the sick can drain you emotionally; beware of burnout if you are making a great many calls. And—a vital preparation and source of strength—keep your personal relationship with God in order, not permanently on vacation while you busy yourself with duties and good deeds.

Do not try to make people feel guilty for being sick or dying. Unfortunately there are some who use a hospital visit as a time to tell a patient that illness or accidents result from some sinful act. Theologically we believe that all people are sinful and that, as Luther noted, everything we do is tainted with sin—but it must be noted that no one's sickness is the result of special sinfulness.

When making institutional visits it is sometimes helpful to gain information from doctors, nurses, or attendants about the person's condition. This is an opportunity for you to find out their suggestions for helping the patient or resident; they can tell you, for example, if he or she has been depressed, very lonely, and so on. Do not ask a patient about the diagnosis or prognosis. It is better to ask, "How are things going?" or use a similar open-ended question.

Make use of chaplains. They can make visits when you cannot, alert you to problems that exist, and obtain information about a patient or resident that you might otherwise be unable to learn. They can also act as advocates for the patient with the medical or nursing home staff.

With many (but not all) people, *openly acknowledging the urine bag, the artificial leg, and so on, helps relieve any embarrassment* or emotional discomfort caused by such conditions.

Don't bring the sick or shut-in your diseases; if you have the flu, stay home.

Calls on the sick or shut-in can be expected or unannounced. Each way has its advantages and disadvantages. Do remember that, for an especially lonely or bored patient, your visit is probably eagerly anticipated. It usually is best, and always polite, to telephone a shut-in at home before you stop by. Advance notice to nursing home staff may be beneficial—especially if the resident will need assistance with personal grooming.

Try not to show horror or shock in your face when you first see a person who is disfigured or has a foul-smelling cancer or other extreme condition. Do not pretend it doesn't exist; just try to be undisturbed by it and focus on the person's needs. If you have difficulty with such situations, desensitize yourself by gradually increased exposures. Practice being relaxed in your visits, making your physical movements smooth and not sharp or jerky; doing everything just a little more slowly than you normally would may help you become more relaxed.

Try not to apologize for not coming sooner or oftener. An apology generally requires some form of response from the other person.

The ill or shut-in frequently like variety and change; a little surprise is always nice. Occasionally drop in at an unusual time; wear something bright or humorous like a Hawaiian shirt; bring a library book, record, or inexpensive gift, and so on.

Visiting the sick is no time to tell other "horror stories" you have heard, such as Aunt Tillie who "had the same thing, God rest her soul."

Do a lot of listening. Sometimes a sick or bereaved person wants nothing more than someone with whom they feel comfortable, who will sit with them and be present without much talk.

Don't play doctor. Do not answer medical questions such as, "When will I get well?" or "How serious is it?" A patient who wants specific information on his or her condition can be urged to make a list of questions to ask the physician; you can also remind a patient that a second medical opinion is available. You can then respond to the feelings of fear or uncertainty that underlie these questions.

When using Scripture, *keep in mind that the Lord's Prayer, Psalm 23, or other portions that are well known to the person are frequently among the most meaningful passages you can mention.* Scripture does not necessarily have to be introduced into the conversation. You can simply make certain that scriptural materials are made available if the individual wants to read from the Bible.

Demonstration

Talking and sharing experiences of hospital, nursing home, and shut-in visitation can be edifying for the leader and trainees. A demonstration will further dramatize what has been covered. After reviewing the suggestions for sick and shut-in visitation, the leader can act out a sample visit to, for example, an elderly church member in a nearby nursing home. Such a role play (lasting about ten minutes) with a class member playing the part of the elderly resident will let trainees visualize the situations and suggestions that have been discussed.

The class is allowed to talk about the demonstration, but the leader must be careful not to let them drag their comments out, because it is important that they have time to practice role playing doing nursing home visits themselves.

Role Play

Gathering into groups of three (one member playing the lay pastoral carer, one the elderly resident, and one acting as an impartial observer), the trainees now have an opportunity to role play a scene similar to the following one.

> The lay caregiver drops in on Mrs. June Lovett, a lifelong member of the church, who is now eighty-four and has been in the nursing home for the five years since her husband died. She has only one surviving child, a son, who is a cabinetmaker in a distant city. Most of Mrs. Lovett's friends and neighbors have died or are no longer able to visit her. She has some friends in the nursing home but still longs for times past when she was able to live in her own house and get around freely. Mrs. Lovett has always been active in the church, except during her twenties, and recently her faith has become deeper and stronger. She thoroughly enjoys the visits from church members.

The leader may wish to suggest other situations that will suit the particular group. When the role play is completed and has been discussed thoroughly by the three, roles are exchanged among them and the same or a similar enactment ensues. Class members are urged to raise their hands if they have questions or get stuck. The leader circulates around the room, answering questions and intervening in any role play that is bogged down or off-target. This is an important opportunity for the leader to give individual guidance to class members; it is a time of intense personal interaction and ought not to be neglected in favor of such activities as reading notes concerning what is to be accomplished next.

At the completion of this practice session, some full-class discussion may be beneficial. The leader can use the time to positively reinforce and applaud class members for the efforts they have made.

This session may be the most practical of the eight, but it deals with a ministry that also may be the most tragically overlooked of any the lay pastoral carer will encounter—and potentially the most meaningful and personally rewarding as well. Hospital, nursing home, and shut-in visitation reaches a group of people who are singularly lonely and cut off from the rest of the world. Even the hospitalized who have family and friends are separated from the vital nourishment provided by one's own *place*. Nursing home residents are often prey to frustration, depression, and utter hopelessness, seeing their situation as the last step in a journey toward death. Ironically, their very isolation hinders them from receiving the caring they so poignantly need. Lay pastoral carers bring their ministry of love and presence right to the bedside—not unlike the good shepherd who, not waiting for the lost to return, goes out after them and seeks relentlessly until they are found and restored to the flock.

8

Care in
Situations of Grief

SESSION 5

☐ Movie on grief (20–30 minutes)
☐ Presentation of the dynamics of grief and ministry to the bereaved (60–75 minutes)
 1. Discussion of and response to the movie
 2. Group sharing of personal grief experiences and what specifically was helpful
 3. Detailing of the dynamics of grief
 4. Brainstorming and discussion of ways in which group members can assist the bereaved
☐ Role play of caring for a recently bereaved person (30 minutes)

HOMEWORK
 1. Continue visiting the same people in nursing homes, making notes after each visit of questions to raise in class.
 2. Read chapter 9 of *The Caring Church*.

When I present the course this book describes to groups of ministers, I am frequently asked why grief is included in the lay pastoral care program. The question is, essentially, "Isn't grief too troubling a subject to cover in a program that you are trying to keep elementary?"

An important reason for dealing with grief in lay pastoral care training is that it is the subject most requested by participants. Virtually all lay pastoral care trainees (and all adults, for that matter) have encountered death among their own families, friends, neighbors, or colleagues. Their widespread discomfort at not knowing what to do and feeling helpless when faced with great loss led me to include this topic area as a regular part of the courses.

Talking about grief also serves as a good personal learning experience for trainees, and the discussion that follows the movie shown at the beginning of the session frequently is a sharing time of some depth. I do not believe people ought to be forced to talk about grief, but once they start exploring the subject it may actually be difficult to get some trainees to stop long enough for the inclusion of some didactic presentations together with the sharing. (In fact, it will be necessary for the group's leader to keep in mind that lay pastoral care training is not group therapy, and that an individual who begins sharing too deeply, in a way that is inappropriate to the teaching process and does not allow for follow-up, needs to be gently stopped. The leader will have a chance later for individual follow-up with the person.)

A final reason for discussing grief, bereavement, and death in a lay pastoral training program is that the grief reaction is actually a prototype for reactions to *all* crises. In other words, carers who understand well the dynamics of grief will be able to help people experiencing a variety of losses. (Other loss reactions can be such things as divorce, loss of job, the "empty nest," loss of physical mobility from an auto accident, moving to a new part of the country—even a dramatic weight loss or a big promotion!) Although most losses tend to have a less intense impact on people than loss by death, the pattern of grief is substantially the same.

A Movie

One very effective way to grasp the impact of grief, both intellectually and emotionally, is to watch and listen to people who have lost a loved one. A twenty- to thirty-minute film in which one or several people share what it was like to lose a spouse, a child, or others close to them, and relate what was and was not helpful in their bereavement, may be shown at this point in the session. Several that I have used are "The Death of a Wished-for Child," "Begin with Goodbye: A Time to Cry," "When a Child Dies," and "Where Is Dead?"

Further information concerning films can be obtained from *Death Education: Audio-Visual Sourcebook*[2] or the National Research and Information Center.[3] One may also contact a local funeral director or the executive director of your state's Funeral Directors Association; they may own films that can be borrowed at little or no cost.

Discussion and Personal Sharing

The balance of session 5 is devoted to a discussion of the film and of grief in general and the offering of specific suggestions about what help can be extended during the grieving process. It usually takes very few suggestions from the leader before people begin talking freely about what they learned, felt, and experienced while viewing the film; there may even be some moist eyes. A few well-timed questions are appropriate, such as, "Was the way the person in the film experienced the loss similar to a grief of your own or someone close to you?" "Did the film remind you of some of your past or present griefs?" "Were there things during your grief that were helpful to you that the person in the film did not mention?"

In addition to the sharing of impressions about grief from the film and from personal experiences, two areas of didactic input are critical. The first is an examination of the specific dynamics of grief; the second is brainstorming some possible ways of responding to people in times of bereavement. It is my experience that both issues will arise as a part of the discussion, and you need to do little more than stop for a few moments to comment on them specifically before going on to further conversation. I would suggest, however, that the leader not move into these didactic presentations too early—it will tend to cut off the personal sharing that people need and want. I prefer to allow the reporting of personal experiences and questioning to go on for at least twenty or thirty minutes before making any formal presentations.

Dynamics of Grief

The first didactic instruction by the leader regards the typical features of a person's normal response to the death of someone close. A one- or two-page synopsis of the dynamics may be handed out to class participants during the ensuing discussion. Several books are available that also can be helpful resources in this regard.[4]

The dynamics of grief presented below were developed through my own counseling practice. Specifically, they grew out of research

I performed a few years ago at the Los Angeles Suicide Prevention Center among widowed spouses in Los Angeles County.[5]

The seven dynamics of grief are: shock, catharsis, depression, guilt, preoccupation with the loss, anger, and adapting to reality. They do not necessarily occur in a linear progression; thus, one who comes through the experience of catharsis does not automatically go next to depression. But the dynamics are to be regarded as seven *major elements* of the typical process of adapting to a great loss and are listed according to the order in which they generally appear.

Shock

In the first few hours and occasionally for the following two weeks or so after the death, the bereaved experience periods of shock. Often the pain of separation is so intense that the mind is numbed until later, when the loss can be accepted better. An individual may act as if nothing happened or behave in a wooden manner while planning the funeral. In a way, shock is the mind's natural anesthetic against the enormity and depth of pain that the loss has caused.

Catharsis (Release of Emotion)

The period of shock is usually short, although it may recur off and on, and the releasing of emotions begins. The immensity of the loss begins to grip the bereaved, and as one emotion surfaces others follow in a flood. Some people become hysterical; others express feelings less openly but experience them just as deeply. Although crying is a common way of expressing grief, in our society it is generally easier for women to cry than it is for men, and it should not be assumed that one who has not wept openly is not "catharting." We need to let the bereaved feel free to express their emotions in their own ways. At the same time we ought not to be frightened when strong feelings come out; it is a normal, healthy part of grief.

Survivors often want a good amount of time alone during this period and may resent company that is forced upon them. One man explained, "They kept saying you have to have people with you. I said no. I've got to face these ghosts. I've got to live in this house. Let me work it out." In short, those who are mourning must have the opportunity to choose whether or not to talk with others.

Depression

After the funeral is over and acquaintances have gone back to "business as usual," the survivors face depression, despair, even thoughts of suicide. Periods of depression are especially prevalent during the first six months, then seem to come and go with diminishing frequency and duration thereafter. Most say this melancholy comes in waves, as bouts of depression occurring without warning, and seems to almost possess them for some time before passing.

Psychosomatic changes (bodily symptoms) also occur as a result of the emotional distress, and dramatic physical disturbances can occur during the grief process. When depression is dominant, there appears to be even more physical distress, illness, "nervousness," and the like. The bereaved ought to be reassured that grief is an emotion, and like all emotions naturally involves physical changes.

Guilt

Feeling guilty is inevitable after a loss by death. Questions such as "Could I have done more for Mom before she died?" regularly arise, and guilt over something said or done to the deceased is common. People often dwell on painful events or angry words, reliving the scenes and wishing they had acted differently. Here also is the possibility that guilt—usually viewed as a negative emotion—can be positive, leading individuals to become more thoughtful and tender in their treatment of others. Whether guilt is about real or imagined events, it is a consistent part of bereavement and requires sensitivity and understanding.

Preoccupation with the Loss

The survivors can become obsessed with thoughts about the deceased. This is not a constant condition, but it ebbs and flows. One may at times function normally and, at others, seem unable to concentrate on anything. By the time outsiders have stopped talking about the one who has died, the preoccupation can manifest itself in guilt-laden ruminations, intense loneliness, sleeplessness, hallucinations about the loved one, or even taking on the behavior and mannerisms of the deceased. All are normal parts of grief; only when the preoccupation becomes an ongoing obsession is it unadaptive.

Anger

When anger is manifested it usually means that one is beginning to come out of depression and preoccupation and is being openly expressive again. Grieving people focus their anger on various individuals and objects—such as doctors, the ambulance driver, the police, or friends and relatives. Their anger can even be leveled at ministers or lay pastoral carers—which may be seen as veiled anger at God. Questions like "Why did God do this to me?" or "How could God let him die?" are often raised by an individual struggling with anger.

It should be noted that the bereaved's anger may also be focused on the deceased, who in effect has "abandoned" the survivor. Such anger is rarely verbalized because the person feels guilty about it and tries to deny such feelings.

Adapting to Reality

In this final dynamic of the grief process, the futility of withdrawal from reality increasingly dawns upon the person, who hopefully now goes on to be a stronger, emotionally healthier person, better able to help others who face the same experience. Reaching the seventh element of grief doesn't mean the bereaved will no longer experience any of the previous dynamics—the individual will struggle with these feelings intermittently for years—but he or she is now open to new possibilities in the present and in the future.

Brainstorming Ways to Help

After the film discussion or the dynamics of grief presentation, usually someone will ask: "But what can *I* do?" I recommend turning the question around by asking: "When you experienced an important grief, what did others do that was helpful to you?" (Or, if you are dealing with a relatively young group that may not have experienced grief to any extent: "If someone close to you were to die, what do you think would be helpful to you?")

The group's suggestions can be listed on the board. The movie probably will have illustrated a few responses that are and are not helpful. Here I try to emphasize that one of the most important ways of ministering to the bereaved is to practice the normal lay pastoral caring skills—attending, listening, responding, and so on. Grief does not necessarily have to be treated as a totally different stress; the warm, tender neighborliness of a Christian friend, such as the kind that trainees offer at nursing homes or in their hospital visits, is also appropriate for the bereaved.

Another important thing for trainees to know as they do their brainstorming is that the *time elapsed* since the loss determines what type of care is appropriate. Grief addressed in the first few moments, hours, and days requires a different type of response than grief that is months old. The leader should also stress to the trainees that the grief reaction is not over after the funeral but lasts through subsequent weeks, months, and even years. Vitally important caring can be offered when the "conspiracy of silence" has set in, when acquaintances have returned to their routines and no longer wish to talk about the deceased. Those times are exceedingly lonely for the bereaved, and the care offered is especially appreciated.

A list of things lay pastoral carers can do in times of grief may include such items as: bringing a casserole to the family; extending physical gestures of caring (a hug or a clasped hand when the depth of suffering is beyond words); dropping by the house in the days, weeks, and months after the funeral when others have stopped visiting; asking, "How are you doing now that Peter is gone?" or saying, "I still miss Loretta" (statements that kindle conversation in the months after the funeral); inviting the bereaved to participate with you in church and community activities or a grief support group; and so on.

Grief brings strong emotions to the fore. Even in people who have not cried since childhood or seem to be always calm, intense reactions can surface. Understanding that this is normal and trying to be as comfortable as possible while they discuss their own feelings about bereavement will make the lay pastoral carers key responders to families in the congregation during times of great loss.

9
Case Studies

□ Discussion of the first nursing home visits and review of the various kinds of calls lay pastoral carers have made or will make (90 minutes)
□ Interpretation of the use of religious resources in pastoral care (30 minutes)

HOMEWORK
1. Incorporate religious resources, especially Scripture and/or prayer, in some of the upcoming pastoral care visits.
2. Read chapter 10 of *The Caring Church*.
3. Continue visiting the people in nursing homes.

"Getting down to cases" is an exciting time in the lay pastoral care training program. Questions and comments have a base in reality, not in expectations or imagination. Vague apprehensions give way to specific problems, and future hopes to accomplished joys. Real people whom class members have encountered bring ministry to life and give the learning task a practical bent and a meaningful purpose.

The First Nursing Home Visits

Those first few interviews with residents of nursing homes etch themselves into lay pastoral carers' minds. Anxiety, relief, excitement, or disappointment heighten the significance of these experiences. A question like "Well, how did your first visits go?" will usually bring considerable response; in fact it may be tempting to spend the remainder of this session discussing those first calls. If possible, all who have made visits (usually at least two-thirds of the group) should be allowed to share those experiences. This also gives the leader a chance to answer any specific questions the group members may have about the visits.[1]

Even if class members seem to be responding that their calls were "a piece of cake," it can safely be assumed that some of the trainees had difficulty with at least one resident. More truthful responses can often be elicited by remarking, "My first visits did not all go that easily—I'm sure some of you had people who were hard to talk to, or other concerns. . . ." Thus, the leader makes the observation that not all lay pastoral care is well received, and not all care offered appears to nourish the other. It can be a good opportunity to emphasize that, although we do our best in offering care, we must realize that the Word will be perceived according to God's time and not always in ways we might want or expect.

While discussing the first visits, the trainer needs to make specific suggestions in answer to questions that are raised. The mood ought to be positive, noting what people have done well, with little negative criticism about flaws in the care they offered. It is realistic to expect some class members to do poorly in the visits—not necessarily because they are unskilled or inadequate, but because their nervousness gets in the way of their basic friendliness. With continued experience in making calls they will become more relaxed, and the natural caring they have to offer will be in evidence.

The review of the first nursing home calls will usually elicit questions from class members about relatives, friends, co-workers, neighbors, and so on. After one member has told the class about a nursing home resident who seems to have given up hope, for example, others may pick up on the issue by interjecting, "What do you do with that? I have an aunt who is dying of cancer and she wants to die" or, "There is a guy at work who is out of sorts all the time and doesn't seem to care about anything since his wife left him. What can I say to him?"

For me, this is when the class really gets interesting. Trainees have recovered from any initial shyness and uncertainty about whether they could ever help someone. They have become committed to the task and want to know more specifics. It will be necessary to continue presenting general theory, but frequently their real hunger is for answers to questions like: "How do you talk to someone who wants to commit suicide?" "What can be

done when my boss's sixteen-year-old daughter has run away?" or
"Where do you send someone who wants to get off drugs?"

The leader needs to answer as many of these questions as possible, using other class members to give suggestions if it can be
done. In the continuing effort to communicate to the class that
they have more skills and abilities than they have recognized, it
is best for the leader to answer a question with a question: "When
you or a close friend had that problem, what helped?" "What do
you suppose would be beneficial?" "How would you handle it?"
This takes considerably more time than answering directly, and
occasionally a less-than-useful suggestion is elicited, but in the
long run it helps the group members to recognize their own
resources and rely upon each other rather than only on the leader.

A good way to reply to many "how-to" queries is to suggest,
"Why don't we role-play the situation? You play the troubled person
and I (or another class member) will be the lay pastoral carer."
Using demonstrations and letting trainees enact specific problems
they have encountered helps the class not only hear but also
visualize various methods of intervention.

Responding to how-to or what-do-you-say questions is appropriate and required of the leader. But there is the danger that both
teacher and participants may get bogged down in tools, techniques,
and methods and lose sight of the most important thing we have
to share: our *selves*. God's enrichment of our own lives is something
that is felt, in our ministry of presence, and that central aspect of
lay pastoral care should not be buried under excessive emphasis
on techniques.

Religious Resources in Lay Pastoral Care

At some earlier point in the teaching of this course—usually after
an extensive talk about the importance of listening and not being
too intrusive or judgmental while establishing the pastoral care
relationship—someone will probably have raised the question,
"We're Christians—how do we witness to people?" or, "Shouldn't
we read the Bible and pray with them?" Usually I try to allay this
concern by noting that the subject of religious resources will be
specifically discussed in the sixth session.

People's views about the use of Scripture, prayer, or talk of God
in pastoral care visits can be quite strong. The following statements

are likely to be seen as gross generalizations, but they note a serious concern about the use of spiritual resources. Lay persons from relatively "conservative" orientations sometimes have such a strong commitment to *witness* that they may do it prematurely, before an effective relationship is established. Such a witness can be mechanistic—"If you do [or believe] such-and such, then you will be saved"—and misses the nuances of an individual's pain. On the other hand, those from the more liberal orientations, not wishing to be thought of as "fundamentalists," may be shy about using Scripture, prayer, and other traditional resources—thus neglecting their potential for offering solace and nourishment. Both sides fail to acknowledge that God comes to humans through both the *spoken Word* and the *visible Word*.[2]

The spoken Word is heard in the sermon, through witnessing, Scripture reading, teaching, and so on. The visible Word is communicated in many ways—through images, the sacraments, helping acts like feeding the poor, and the ministry of presence mentioned earlier. The danger of the "conservative" is to overemphasize the spoken Word and ignore the visible Word; whereas the "liberal" offering pastoral care may overlook the spoken Word in dwelling on the visible Word. Both need to be incorporated into the care that is offered; emphasizing one to the exclusion of the other limits the degree to which one's ministry can be a channel for the Word of God to bring comfort, strength, reconciliation, and renewal to the other.

Since each religious heritage stresses different resources, the sixth session must be tailored to the group's particular tradition. Questions regarding such things as private Communion by lay persons, the use of occasional services in lay pastoral care, "emergency" baptism, and so on can be discussed where they are appropriate. Universal issues to be addressed are the use of Scripture and the use of prayer—both of which have been major contributors to spiritual growth throughout the centuries.

Scripture

Each leader will emphasize certain aspects of Scripture as a "lamp . . . and a light" (Ps. 119:105) to the troubled. A few suggestions I find helpful in the application of Scripture for lay pastoral care visitation are as follows.

Listen carefully to the concerns expressed and then choose portions of Scripture that address the center of a person's specific need. To one overwrought with guilt, for example, passages that confront sin are not appropriate, but words of 1 John 1:9 may suffice: "If we confess our sins, God who is faithful and just, will forgive our sins and cleanse us from all unrighteousness."

Scripture can be a source of sustenance during difficult times. Sharing from the psalms and other passages that express the pain, suffering, and sorrow we all encounter as human beings helps one to recognize that others also have experienced deep pain, and that God is with us and speaks to us in times that try our patience and our faith.

During crises people regress emotionally. At such times, the most beneficial Scripture excerpts frequently are "old favorites" such as Psalm 23, John 3:16, or the Lord's Prayer.[3] When there is a death or a great loss, familiar passages almost always are the most appreciated.

In some instances, *characters from the Bible can be cited to illustrate certain ways of acting.* Narrative passages and the parables are good sources for such examples.

Although the Bible's message of God's intervention in human life is always the same, various authors of Scripture have expressed the event in different ways and out of different cultures and belief systems. Therefore, it is possible for people to reach odd or confused interpretations of what God wants for their lives.[4] *Gentle confrontation and correction of such misinterpretation may be necessary.* There are some, for example, who believe Christ died on the cross for everyone but themselves, and a reminder of the sixteenth verse of the third chapter of John helps to clear their thinking. (Personally sharing "what John 3:16 has meant to me" is more effective than saying, "This is what you ought to believe.")

Be familiar with Scripture. One of the thrusts of the Reformation was to give the Scriptures back to the people, but in recent years some of the laity have given the Scriptures back to the clergy—and unfortunately some parish clergy have passed them back to their seminary professors. This trend must be reversed if pastoral care is to be implemented.

A final suggestion: *arguing about the meaning of Scripture is not usually a good idea.* It may be appropriate to express a different understanding of some issue by quoting from the Bible, but do it very gently. If the person begins to argue, it is best to say "uncle" and move on. Times of stress or crisis are not times for debate, and such a use of Scripture will only create resistance.

Prayer

Christ's ministry ought to serve as an influence on the use of prayer in one's own pastoral care ministry. He found the need to go away by himself and pray, and he gave us ways and forms for how best to pray: the Lord's Prayer. The following petition of Martin Luther is an eloquent response to Jesus' example, and gives further insights into an attitude of prayer that seeks God's strength and guidance and remains open to the Spirit's direction.

> O my dear Lord Jesus Christ, you have said: Ask, and it will be given to you; seek, and you shall find; knock, and it shall be opened unto you. In keeping with this promise, give to me, Lord. I ask neither gold nor silver, but for a strong and firm faith. While I seek let me find not lust and pleasure of the world, but comfort and refreshment through your blessed and healing word. Open to me, while I knock. I desire nothing which the world cherishes, for by it I would not be uplifted even for so much as the breadth of a hair. Grant me your Holy Spirit, who enlightens my heart, and comforts and strengthens me in my cares and trials. He secures my right faith and trust in your grace to the very end. Amen.[5]

Listed below are six suggestions for facilitating the use of prayer in lay pastoral care. The leader may wish to add to or delete from these ideas.

Prayer is not manipulation. Its purpose is not to make God do what you want—or, for that matter, to get the person being helped to do what you think is best. Nor is it a time for persuasion. The style of the Lord's Prayer is one that still provides a good example of the form prayer can best take.

Use the language of the person you are caring for in spoken petitions. A prayer will be more understandable to the one in need and more of a shared experience if its phrases are congruent with the individual's world, rather than with a liturgical or "King James" style (unless the person prefers that terminology). This is not to say that you should outdo the adolescent with "hip" terms—just try to speak in a language that is understandable. And do not affect a "prayer voice"; speak in your natural conversational tone.

Keep prayers short, especially with a very sick person. Prayers and homilies are not to be confused.

When asked to pray, say "I'd be happy to. What concerns do you wish to lay at the Lord's feet?" or, "Let's do. What are the things you want to share?" This can take off the pressure when you don't know what to say and helps the other identify and articulate various needs and concerns. When a person is finished sharing what he or she wants to tell God, it is sometimes appropriate to ask, "Would you like to join me by beginning the prayer, and letting me finish?"

Prayer may be used at any time during a visit but seems most fitting at the end or as a response to crucial points in the conversation. It is *not* a requirement for every pastoral care visit and need only be used when requested or when the lay person deems it appropriate. Prayer is especially appreciated at times of illness, impending death, and grief; as a response to felt guilt; and as an expression of joy and gratitude.

Whether you pray or not during each pastoral care visit, *it is important to remember in your own private prayers all of the people you see.* A vital part of the preparation for and debriefing after a pastoral call is seeking God's strength and wisdom in your own personal ministry.[6]

In the process of giving pastoral care to a troubled individual, the lay minister will need time and time again to draw upon the resources of a rich spiritual life, the strength and guidance available through Scriptures and prayer, and a close relationship with God.

10
Problem Solving and Referral

SESSION 7

- ☐ Discussion and practice of how to help people solve problems (40–60 minutes)
- ☐ Consideration of methods of referral (60 minutes)
    1. How to refer
    2. Listing of local referral sources
- ☐ Class role play of problem-solving or referral situations (as time allows)

HOMEWORK

1. Select from the following options:
    a. make contact with several of the listed referral agencies to learn more about their services; or
    b. practice problem solving with one of your own problems.
2. Continue visiting the assigned people in nursing homes.
3. Read chapter 11 of *The Caring Church.*

Corrine McConnell is assistant director of the research department in a large manufacturing company. She participated in her church's lay pastoral care training program and found the skills she learned particularly useful when one of the research chemists, Anne Peretti, began making uncharacteristic mistakes and missing work frequently. Corrine invited Anne to lunch, and in the course of their conversation Anne revealed that the cause of her instability was a series of serious and (to her) distressing conflicts with her widowed mother, with whom Anne had been living ever since she finished college.

It was not necessary for Corrine to establish a relationship with Anne since they worked together and knew each other well. (This may often be the case for lay pastoral carers.) And Anne seemed to have a good grasp of her problem. Her mother, whose health was poor, had become increasingly demanding of her daughter's time and allegiance. She was jealous of Anne's friends—especially her male friends—and clearly feared that if Anne became more independent, she herself would be left alone and forgotten. This was in spite of Anne's frequent protests that she loved her mother and would continue to visit and be involved with her—even if she were to get married or for any reason move out of the house (something Anne wanted very much to do).

But understanding the problem clearly was not enough. The arguments had become more and more frequent, and Mrs. Peretti had started using her illness to control almost all of Anne's spare time. Anne did not want to abandon her mother, whom she loved very much and to whom she had once been close, and so she felt trapped in an unsolvable situation.

Corrine had a pretty clear picture of the problem by the time the two of them finished their soup, and when the salad arrived they were already discussing what Anne would consider to be desirable and realistic goals for resolving the conflict. They had begun listing resources Anne could call upon when it was time to go back to work, and it was already evident that some of Anne's most important resources in this particular situation would be her mother's younger sister and two of her mother's oldest friends, all of whom lived alone but maintained contact with their children.

Corrine had a business luncheon the following day, but the pair agreed to meet at noon in two days to continue their discussion. In the meantime, Anne would add to the list of resources both for herself and for her mother and would identify each one with a note about ways in which it could be used to help (however remote). The two women had also begun discussing possible alternative courses of action (Corrine suggested two that occurred to her immediately but that Anne had not thought of in the midst of her distress over the emotional arguments she and her mother had been having). By 1:15, only slightly late back to her work station, Anne already felt that a load had been lifted from her shoulders and realized that what had seemed an impossible dilemma was in fact resolvable.

By the time of their next meeting, Anne had completed a list of resources which she narrowed to her mother's small circle of friends, her mother's lately neglected interest in animal welfare (she had helped found the city's humane society years before), and her adequate if not extravagant income from her parents' estate. Anne had already decided to ask her mother's sister and one of her close friends to talk to Mrs. Peretti about how well they managed living alone and how faithful their children had been in maintaining contact. Anne also would ask them to spend time with Mrs. Peretti during the transition period when and if she decided to get her own apartment. The financial resources would provide a visiting nurse or companion should Mrs. Peretti's health require that kind of care.

After discussing with Corrine the pros and cons of the alternatives available to her, Anne decided that every course of action that involved remaining in her mother's house would only prolong their conflict. She would begin looking for an apartment immediately, enlist the help of her mother's sister and friends in the transition, and patiently "wait out" the inevitable upsets that would occur upon her leaving—with the belief that, in time, her mother would see she was not going to abandon her.

Anne felt relieved about making the decision, but she was nervous about telling her mother. Corrine suggested that she ask her aunt to be present for moral support, that she find ways of demonstrating her continued caring for her mother, and that she refuse to be part of any repetitious arguments.

Corrine also offered to be available for "backup," if the predictable fight became too upsetting for Anne and she felt herself weakening.

Anne promised to have the talk with her mother that night or the next—as soon as her aunt was free—and to let Corrine know by Friday what had happened.

As it turned out, Anne's mother did create a terrible scene, and there were many tears, threats, and accusations. It was painful for Anne, but because she and Corrine had *predicted* it and planned how Anne would deal with it, her resolve held. Within ten days she found an apartment that she liked and could afford, and two weeks later the move was completed.

Anne began calling her mother three times a week and visiting her every Thursday night. The first few calls and visits were difficult until a pattern had been established and Mrs. Peretti could begin to trust her daughter's promises. Anne had talked with the director of the humane society, who was delighted to ask Mrs. Peretti for help with a fund-raising campaign among people in the community whom she had known for decades. This not only gave her a meaningful task, it also led to the renewal of friendships that she had neglected in her excessive dependence upon her daughter.

Until the ups and downs of the move evened out and Anne was able to get her relationship with her mother back on an even keel, Corrine continued to be available for support and review of the actions Anne had taken. Anne's work returned quickly to its normal high quality, and what was more, she was able to apply her newly learned skills in problem solving to any number of more routine problems in her work and her life.

Problem Solving

The ultimate goal of all helping is *action*—whether it be making a decision, accepting a loss that cannot be changed, learning a new skill, finding a job, or something else. Thought-out and decisive action leads to growth.

The seventh session makes the point that in *some* lay caring it is important to go beyond listening and help the person make decisions that can be acted upon. (One decision may even be referral to a specialized helping professional.) This is the C of the ABC crisis intervention method referred to previously.

Knowing what the problem is but being unable to find a solution is a common difficulty, yet it is useless to boil down the problem if no action is going to be taken. Each lay pastoral carer requires a systematic model or models that can be used in assisting people to weigh alternatives, make decisions, and take the first steps toward problem resolution. Problem-solving methods are based on the assumption that merely communicating a problem and expressing your feelings about it are not always sufficient. In some cases the problem persists (such as the alcoholic husband who continues beating his wife whenever he drinks) until the person takes action and begins to make responsible choices.

There are a variety of problem solving methods in existence.[1] The following five-step approach is one I have adapted and found effective in helping an individual move from *talking* about a problem to *doing something* about it.

Goals

Changing the focus of the helping from negative (problems) to positive (goals) is the first step in problem solving. Once some general, long-term goals are stated, it is important to develop specific, short-term, easily attained objectives toward which the problem solving will be aimed. For example, if the problem is that a void was left when a couple's last daughter married an Air Force pilot and moved to another country, the *goal* is to find new tasks and meaning now that the nest is empty and only long distance parenting is required; one *objective* may be to start up that mail order business they had talked about for years but never seemed to have time to put in operation.

Resources

Next it is essential to take an inventory of those internal resources (inner strengths and skills, past successes in problem solving, special abilities, methods of coping, etc.) as well as external or environmental resources (friends, church, school, finances, etc.) that can be brought to bear upon resolving the current problem. The inventory should also list how each item can be used, such as for enjoyment and companionship, spiritual sustenance, medical attention, and so on. The question to be asked during the inventory of resources is "What does this person have in her or his life that can assist in attaining the desired goals?"

Alternatives

After establishing goals and objectives and cataloging resources, it is time to brainstorm the possibilities available for reaching a solution. List *all* of the alternatives—the wacky as well as the plausible. It may be necessary for the pastoral carer to start or assist in the list development to show the individual (whose thinking may be clouded) how many courses of action are indeed possible. However, it is better if most of the ideas can come from the person with the problem.

The brainstorm list then can be narrowed and the obviously inappropriate alternatives weeded out. Since several courses of action may achieve the same goal, it is necessary to consider other things the person is trying to accomplish in attaining the change. The individual's ethics and moral code are to be considered as you sift through possible actions. Work schedule, family obligations, finances, and so on may have a bearing as well. It is crucial to choose those alternatives that most effectively accomplish good and are congruent with the person's values.

After the initial elimination process, the relative effectiveness of the remaining courses of action is weighed. Here you can provide information out of your own experiences and background that might help the individual evaluate how well each alternative will aid in reaching the desired goals and objectives. In some cases a combination of two or more alternatives may be just the ticket for resolving the situation; therefore, no single idea should be dismissed too quickly. The listing and selecting of alternatives is a collaborative effort in which lay pastoral carer and troubled individual together choose those that are most likely to be effective. The emphasis will of course be on the individual taking as much responsibility and initiative as possible.

Commitment to Action

When the list of alternatives is narrowed to one or a few that have a high chance of success, the person has to make a firm commitment to embark upon the chosen course(s). The action may (and often should) be broken down into very small, concrete, easily attained steps.

O. Hobart Mowrer once wrote, "It is easier to act your way into a new way of *feeling* than to feel your way into a new way of *acting.*"[2] Certainly taking action is essential in problem solving, but it is often the point at which people balk and put up resistance. They may forget to do what they decided to do, or become too busy. They may be afraid of the consequences of a change in their way of functioning. It is the lay pastoral carer's task to encourage an individual in any way possible to begin *doing,* because only then can positive change occur and (as Mowrer noted) can the person begin feeling better. If resistance persists at this point, referral is in order.

Review and Refinement

Once concrete steps are taken to resolve the problem, review and refinement become a conscious part of the problem-solving process. A constant evaluation of the effectiveness of the new steps taken in achieving the chosen goals and objectives is essential. In some cases the goals themselves may need evaluation and even alteration: they may be unrealistic, or the individual may find that other goals have become more important as the change process has proceeded.

When the class presentation of the five steps of problem-solving has been completed, including suggestions from trainees of ways in which they solve problems, if time allows an exercise may be used (if not here, then after referral is discussed). Lay pastoral carers may examine and evaluate their own problem solving methods or they may participate in a role-play situation. In the former case the leader may suggest an imaginary problem for them to solve (for example, you are overweight and want to reduce; or your spouse died and you are lonely)—or better, suggest they tackle an existing problem of their own or rework one they recently addressed. I urge them to work alone for ten to fifteen minutes and then share their problems and how they would resolve them with a group of four or five people. The small group gives feedback and frequently provides encouragement actually to do the chosen action.

Alternately, a role-play situation similar to the case at the beginning of this chapter can be assigned and worked on in groups of three. The task of the trainee playing the carer will be to assist the other to make his or her own decision.

Referral

It has been my experience that the major reason why helpers of all sorts—lay pastoral carers, pastors, even psychologists and marriage and family counselors—do not refer is that they do not know where or how to refer. These two issues need to be covered in the training. Pastoral carers must understand that *the need to refer does not mean they are inadequate or unskilled.* On the contrary; referral is vital in all helping and especially in pastoral care, and knowing how to refer effectively is a crucial skill for all trainees to learn.

In one form of referral, the lay minister continues the contact and remains primarily responsible for the person's care but suggests a specialist of some type to assist the helping process. Such a specialist may be, for example, a lawyer, a family debt counselor, a person skilled in relaxation training through biofeedback, or a self-help group like Alcoholics Anonymous or Gamblers Anonymous.

However, when the troubled individual is seriously suicidal or homicidal, exhibits personality disorder or psychosis, or requires hospitalization or medication, or when psychological counseling is needed, the major responsibility is shifted to a professional skilled in the type of care required. This does not necessarily end the relationship, however; the pastoral carer continues to show concern as a friend while the person receives treatment elsewhere. Nobody is "dumped."

Referral to an outside source often is inevitable and never should be viewed as a sign of failure. In fact, knowing when to refer is a mark of a good carer. You need to be aware of your own limitations—the time you have available, your skill, your emotional objectivity, and so on—to determine if and when it is best to send the individual you are visiting to receive professional care.

Three questions should be asked to determine if referral would be beneficial—questions of time, skill, and emotional objectivity.

Do I have enough time? Granted that you possess the necessary helping skills for assisting with a particular individual's problem, it is necessary to determine if your available time is sufficient to adequately deal with the situation. Will your other responsibilities be neglected because of the time and energy this individual's problems will require of you? Or can you impose limitations without cost to the person's healing process?

Are my skills sufficient? Granted that your available time is sufficient, it is also important to know if your own skills and experience are adequate to the task, or if a pastor, counselor or therapist would be of more benefit to the individual. (In the case of serious drug addiction, for example, very few lay persons—or even ministers or family therapists—are equipped with the knowledge or facilities for treating it effectively.)

If you are not certain whether you have adequate skills to deal with a particular individual, you might ask yourself: Does this person make me feel uncomfortable? Is he or she showing growth?

Do I understand the individual's situation clearly? Is the person becoming excessively dependent upon me?

(The above questions apply to relatively "normal" problem situations; as already mentioned, referral is *always* indicated in cases of psychosis, violent behavior, serious suicide or homicide threats, or any noticeably bizarre actions.)

Can I remain emotionally neutral? Assuming your time is sufficient and your skills adequate to handle a particular problem, it is important to examine your own emotional objectivity. There may be some situations which—because of your own beliefs and moral code or your own past difficulties in resolving the same problems—arouse within you feelings of insecurity or hostility, threat or fear. Is this problem one that you yourself have faced but never successfully resolved? Are you so overburdened emotionally that you have little left to offer this individual? Do you find yourself needing the other's approval so that it is difficult to intervene with integrity and authority? Or are you finding yourself becoming overly emotionally involved with the person or the situation?

In every phase of the care process, whether in establishing a relationship, working out a course of action, or referring to a specialist, the lay pastoral carer's effective functioning depends upon the degree to which she or he understands all of the limitations of the situation and acts creatively out of a sense of emotional security, stability, and relative objectivity. I have been impressed over the years with the quality of referral work offered by truck drivers, career women, students, and other lay people working on crisis telephone lines. With the assistance of capable supervisors and ready access to sources of referral they are able to make sound, accurate referrals. In the case of lay pastoral carers, their pastors, other church members who are mental health professionals, local crisis "hot lines," or information and referral services can provide the support and supervision for referral that is needed. When referral is required, the following ideas may apply. The leader may add to this list from her or his own experience.

Don't assume that everyone will accept your suggestions for referral. Some may only want to complain about a situation and not work toward a solution. For others, just talking about the problem and considering a referral is sufficient to motivate them to action.

Make referrals in a concrete way: not "I think you should see a shrink" but "There are several marriage counselors I'd be happy to recommend. Dr. Brown was especially helpful with my sister and I've heard very good things about Dr. Thistlethwaite from several people who have seen her."

When you are uncertain of where a person should be referred, call your pastor, a local crisis line, or an information and referral agency and explain the situation. In this way you will get up-to-date information on the person or agency to which you are referring. You may even wish to call the person or office and find out if they have a waiting list, how long it is, and any other information that may be useful.

Suggest several referral sources (if possible), since one professional may have a long waiting list or be unavailable at present.

Do not make the referral call for a person you are helping (except in an emergency). Have the individual initiate the call. It may be good for you to suggest dialing the number *now,* using your telephone, or to offer a ride (if you are willing) to the first appointment.

Remember, referral is not the first thing you do (except in an emergency) in the care you offer. Establish a relationship, listen carefully to the person's pain, and then slowly, gently begin to nudge toward doing something about the problem, noting how the suggested referral source can benefit in the resolution.

After referring, follow up. Call the next day and explain in a nonjudgmental way, "I called to see how you are today, and to find out if there were any problems in scheduling a session with Dr. Brown or Dr. Thistlethwaite." If the person gives excuses or "hasn't had a chance," ask if there are any further ways you can help or if there are other things the individual would like to discuss with you. Mention that you will call back in a couple of days to see how things are going. Do not hound anyone—but do not let a person "get off easily" either.

Up to now the issue has been *how* to refer. After the class members have discussed this component of referral thoroughly, they have to learn *where* to refer. I strongly suggest that the pastor prepare her or his own referral list of those persons or agencies that are helpful and local to the church. Such a list would include, at least: (1) crisis lines and/or information and referral agencies; (2) alcoholism and drug treatment facilities, including Alcoholics

Anonymous; (3) counseling services such as community mental health centers, family service agencies, pastoral counseling centers, and the like; (4) organizations that help children and adolescents, including homes for runaways; (5) legal support offices such as Legal Aid; (6) medical hospitals and the chaplains who work there; (7) problem pregnancy resources; (8) financial counseling services (or a banker who is a member of the congregation) that aid people with money problems; (9) resources for the retarded and handicapped; (10) transportation services for the elderly; (11) support services for women such as temporary shelters or rape crisis centers; and (12) any other resources that are useful and available in your own community.

Further assistance for finding places to refer can be gained from existing referral lists in the community. Some agencies likely to have such lists are: crisis lines, the local mental health association, an information and referral service, pastoral counseling centers, and governmental referral offices. Sometimes these agencies have referral books, pamphlets, or handout sheets that can be used with little or no adaptation. An additional help is a book by Marcus Bryant and Charles Kemp, *The Church and Community Resources*.[3]

It is easy for session 7 to become heavily weighted toward the leader's input. Therefore time must be allowed either after the presentation of problem-solving methods or after the discussion of referral—or both—for the class members to practice their new skills. By now most are quite comfortable in the use of role play, and the leader can design a situation to cover one or both of the issues raised in the session. An episode I have frequently assigned is one in which an alcoholic's husband tells a neighbor that she has come home drunk, again, and he is at his wits' end. The helper has to work at both problem solving and referral (Alanon, AA, counseling, etc.) in the care offered.

The methods presented in session 7 considerably expand the lay pastoral carer's skill vocabulary, as well as increase the quality of ministry and the number of people who can be reached. The carer's use of effective problem-solving techniques not only helps an individual to resolve a present difficulty; it also gives the person new skills for dealing with future problems. And, through referral, the lay minister can become a bridge between the distressed and any specialized help she or he might need—but otherwise avoid—while continuing to provide a caring and supportive presence.

11
Wrapping Up

SESSION 8

☐ Exploration (and possible role play) of potential pastoral care opportunities not previously covered (80 minutes)

☐ Explanation of the structure of lay pastoral care ministry in your church by the group's lay leader (30 minutes)

☐ Evaluation of the lay pastoral care training program (10 minutes)

The ship is about to be launched. Most class members will have mixed feelings—excitement about what lies ahead and sadness about losing the support of the weekly training sessions. By this time many will have questions from the visits they have already made or from past experiences when they did not know how to handle a crisis situation, or will be wondering about how they could have helped someone in their family differently. Now, with the weekly training nearing a close, they feel the pressure to find answers.

It has been my observation that the last session is best kept open-ended. The session may begin with brainstorming, writing on a chalkboard the questions and cases class members would like to discuss. With very little coaxing usually enough issues will be collected to fill three classes! A number of areas arise with great consistency, such as questions on ministry to the dying and be-reaved; how to care for a person who is doing something you believe is wrong (for example, child beating, or failing to report income to the IRS); how to care for someone who wants a divorce or is recently divorced; concerns about people who are suicidal; how to make visits to a church member with AIDS; what to do when a teenager runs away; the handling of older parents who live with their children or may need to go to a nursing home; how to care for a family with an Alzheimer's disease patient. The questions raised by each group will of course vary from this listing—but you will usually get most of these and many more.

After the list of topics is completed, the class starts considering as many issues as time will allow. There are two tasks in this last session. First, to give the group more practice in role playing, it is helpful if class members enact at least one of the cases or issues (such as how you care for a father who is habitually abusing his two-year-old). A second task is for the trainees to do more of their own thinking, relying upon themselves or other members of the group rather than the "expert" (leader). So when one asks, "What do you do when . . . ?" the teacher asks the class: "What do you think?" or "What did some of you do when this happened to you or a close friend?" It is the leader's duty to begin pulling away somewhat from the expert role and help the class to rely upon each other to a greater extent.

One important concern that typically comes up is suicide. That one issue can paralyze a pastoral carer and, although it will not be encountered by many, can serve to prevent those who fear it from entering the field with any vigor.

Suicide Lethality

One of the most alarming situations a lay pastoral carer can come upon is a person who may be suicidal. Throughout the following discussion it should be remembered that the carer must contact the pastor immediately if there is *any* suspicion or threat that an individual may commit suicide.

A helpful way to "listen for" suicide risk is to make judgments about suicide lethality. The following are a series of items that can help in assessing the suicide potential.[1] These nine basic criteria are not to be used as a checklist but are to be internalized and the answers gained informally (but directly) in conversation with the potentially suicidal person.

Age and Sex

Although 55 percent of completed suicides are men, women attempt suicide more frequently. The threat of suicide increases in lethality with age, especially in the case of men. Therefore, if a retired man and a teenage girl are both threatening suicide, the man is statistically more likely to complete the act—although, of course, all talk of suicide must be treated seriously.

Suicide Plan

The plan is the most critical element in assessing suicide risk. The lay pastoral carer will have to determine how specific the plan is, how lethal the method, and how available the means for putting the plan into effect. The answers to these questions generally will not be available through just listening, but will require direct and forthright questioning of the troubled person. It is obvious that some means of committing suicide are more lethal than others, for example, a gun more than tranquilizers, or a full bottle of barbiturates more than a handful of aspirin. If a person has a very specific plan, has spent time thinking in detail about how he or she will commit the act, has selected a lethal method, and has means readily available, there is a very serious suicide risk. The lay pastoral carer should seek help immediately.

Stress

Most serious threats of suicide occur when an individual is in crisis, brought on by a loss or potential loss such as death, divorce, illness or retirement. If the stress is extreme and the individual has a specific suicide plan, then a very active response is required of the lay pastoral carer.

Symptoms

The completion of the suicide act can come as a result of several different emotional states, among them depression, psychosis, and agitation. The most serious is the depressive-agitated state, in which the person feels emotionally depressed but is simultaneously tense and active and therefore has the energy and determination to complete the act. (Contrary to popular myth, not everyone who commits suicide is depressed.) Furthermore, alcoholics, drug abusers, homosexuals, and sexual deviates have a higher-than-average suicide rate.

Meaning and Religious Involvement

Strong religious beliefs and regular involvement with some church or religious group provide both emotional support and social constraint against suicide. The individual who is neither influenced by nor committed to any religious belief system or group is generally freer to complete the act. However, even highly religious people do commit suicide.

Resources

It is essential to identify relatives, friends, church members, social workers, co-workers, and others who are available to assist the suicidal individual through the crisis (if there is one). Although the person may feel she or he has no resources, that "nobody cares," the pastoral carer knows there are usually more resources available than the individual realizes. Above all, the person should be encouraged to be frank with other people about the seriousness of her or his difficulties; in the case of one who appears suicidal and seems immobilized, it may be a good idea to call some of the resource persons and tell them of the suicide potential so they can become involved and can actively communicate their caring to the person. If the individual considering suicide has few personal resources, then the lay pastoral carer as an extension of the church reaches out to broaden her or his net of resources and provide support for grappling with the present difficulties.

Life-style

A stable life-style is indicated by such things as consistent work history, long marriage and stable family relations, and absence of past suicide activity. Unstable individuals may exhibit chronic alcoholism, job-hopping or marriage-hopping, character disorder or psychosis, frequent unresolved crises, and so on. Chronic suicide threats happen only among unstable personalities, but acute suicidal gestures may occur among people with stable as well as unstable life-styles.

Communication

Communication is vital; the individual who is not communicating with others may have given up hope and is more likely to at least attempt suicide. Indirect nonverbal communication (such as making a new will, giving up prized possessions or favorite activities, etc.) should be considered as well as direct verbal communication; indirect communication rarely reaches the notice of helping professionals and can be difficult to discern. Lay pastoral carers, along with family and friends, may thus be the only ones to notice such signs of distress and provide the pastor or mental health professional with information regarding the lethality of the threat.

Medical Record

The pastoral carer should find out if a suicidal individual has (or fears) a serious disease such as cancer, impending or recent surgery, or chronic illness. More than once people have committed suicide believing they had cancer when in fact they were free of the disease. Furthermore, individuals who have confirmed terminal illnesses may seek suicide as a way of coping.

None of the above criteria, except for a specific and lethal plan, is necessarily dangerous when taken alone. It is important to gather all the information and look at the whole picture to see if a pattern is beginning to form.

A basic underlying rule in dealing with suicide—even the hint of it—is to *take all ideas about suicide seriously.* A person who makes statements like "I'm tired of trying," "Life isn't worth living anymore," or "There is no way out" should be asked directly if she or he is contemplating suicide. It is not true that discussing it will cause the person to do it; talking about suicide, in frank and specific detail so that assistance can be offered, is *much better* than ignoring it. Once again, if anyone is even suspected of being suicidal, the lay pastoral carer must take it seriously and contact the pastor immediately.

Structuring Lay Pastoral Care Ministry

The person who will serve as lay leader of the pastoral carers conducts the last part of this session. Any or all of the following items may be raised.

Class members should be reminded again of the importance of not repeating what someone has said during a visit in conversations with others, not even with their spouses. Lay pastoral carers may consult with the pastor, lay leader, or another lay pastoral carer on a case, but *they must maintain confidentiality* outside that small circle. They also should not discuss *other* group members' cases, probably the most likely place for breaches of confidentiality to occur.

The lay pastoral carers are urged to be initiators in their own ministries. They are not merely to wait for requests from people who want them to visit; they are to reach out to family, friends, neighbors, church members, or co-workers whom they see in need.

Since the first edition of *The Caring Church* was printed, a pattern I have noted in some churches is that newly trained lay pastoral carers become impatient with leaders (clergy and lay) who do not call on them to make visits frequently enough. There appear to be two causes for such a problem. First, the leaders are not using the trained lay pastoral carers to visit a number of existing populations in the church and community such as those in retirement homes, nursing homes, children's hospitals, homes for retarded individuals, missions, or shut-ins in the congregation. Some church leaders think exclusively of crises when they think of lay pastoral care, but there exists in every community a large group of people who are not in crisis but who nevertheless need our care—and they are invisible to most of us in our day to day lives. Secondly, lay pastoral carers themselves at times may be too passive, waiting for problems to come knocking on the door rather than taking initiative, responding to opportunities for care that are all around them. It requires sensitizing our eyes and ears to the people with whom we have daily contact. They are there! It does not take long for others to become aware of our concern and sensitivity.

Class members also have to be informed exactly how people will be assigned to them—whether directly by the pastor or through the lay leader or both.

In order to more effectively assign people in need to the lay ministers, several churches have used a short questionnaire that the class fills out. Whether a formal questionnaire is used or not, the lay leader and pastor should request specifics about how their lay carers are willing and able to accept assignments and what kinds of loads they want and can handle. It is also helpful to know if there are certain situations in which the carers feel uncomfortable or others for which they believe they are especially well-equipped.

All lay pastoral carers must know the ground rules concerning reporting back what happened during assigned calls. They will need to know to whom they should report (pastor, lay leader, or other) and in which cases and what detail they are to explain the outcomes of their visits.

If there are to be regular (for example, monthly) meetings of the lay pastoral care group—which are strongly recommended—the details of such meetings should be covered. Class members are reminded that they can also call the pastor, the lay leader, or other lay pastoral carers to discuss a case at any time if they feel the need. They are urged not to be shy and not to fear showing ignorance in such cases.

If a service of dedication is to be used (see appendix A), the order of the service is covered and questions are answered.

Any additional items concerning the functioning of the ongoing lay ministry group are noted.

Evaluation

It is helpful to close the session with an oral or written evaluation of the training by the class members, which is an effort to improve and refine future training programs. Any form the leader prefers to use will suffice. I typically use an anonymous written form that includes the following questions:

1. My overall assessment of this training program is (a) excellent (b) very good (c) good (d) fair (e) poor. (Circle one.)
2. The most helpful parts of the training were: (be specific).
3. The least helpful parts of the training were: (be specific).
4. I would like to see the following changes when this course is taught in the future:
5. Final comments:

Input from trainees is then integrated, if possible, into the structure of future training sessions.[2]

As the sessions come to an end, pastoral care trainees prepare to embark on that ministry of which all Christians are a part, but with sharpened skills and a heightened understanding of the needs and issues they will meet in the world they are called to serve.

12

New Directions in Lay Pastoral Care

To love and care for others is the new command initiated by the incarnate Word's intervention in our lives. This "law of love" is a foundation for all pastoral care. To quote Romans 13:8-10, "He who loves his neighbor has fulfilled the law . . . love does no wrong to a neighbor; therefore love is the fulfilling of the law."

Jesus, in his radical obedience unto death, revealed on the cross the meaning of love. Victor Furnish expresses this transformed meaning of love by defining it (and I paraphrase) as caring for others—not because of who they are or where they stand in relation to oneself, but just because they exist, and because they are there. It means identifying with them, with their needs, hurts, joys, hopes, lostness and loneliness. It means being willing to risk taking the initiative in reconciliation, and being willing, finally, to give oneself to them in service and support of their humanity.[1]

This book has repeatedly made the point that the ministry of caring is not limited to those with degrees in theology. Pastoral care—one way in which love can be shared—is a task of all Christian people as part of their grateful response to God's love. Each is a member of the universal priesthood, and every Christian has different gifts and abilities to offer—a listening ear for a troubled teenager; information on alcoholism referral; a casserole for a family that has recently experienced a death; a drop-in visit on an eighty-seven-year-old shut-in with no living family.

Many congregants would like to respond to others in acts of caring but shy away because of feelings of incompetence or uncertainty. The eight two- to two-and-a-half-hour weekly training sessions described herein were designed to help lay persons gain the confidence and skills they need to express love and give pastoral

care to others. The training was not intended to create parapro-
fessional pastoral counselors but, rather, to unleash the caring of
those lay people who have experienced the claim of God's love.
The sessions were formulated to give an account of what lay pastoral
care is and to draw a picture of the caring relationship—including
attending, listening, responding, problem solving, and referral.
They also relate the basics of making visits to shut-ins or to hospital
patients, as well as ministering to the bereaved. The final sessions
discuss specific cases and areas of concern with the class members.

The purpose of the book has been to help a congregation get
started in lay pastoral care training. Once the first group has
finished training, they have only begun. In these final paragraphs
I would like to comment on some of what may lie ahead, but this
discussion will be in no way complete.

Since this book was first published, it has become patently clear
that lay pastoral care groups operate best only with the continued
involvement of the pastor or a very committed lay leader or better
both. In some churches I have seen the minister invest great effort
to offer the training, then back off and let the program die. This
happens for several reasons. In some cases the pastor was not really
committed to the idea of lay pastoral care in the first place and
therefore, did not put enough thought or effort into recruitment
(especially recruitment of the lay leaders) and training.

Another reason may be that some pastors end their involvement
with the group as soon as it is launched. Although it is good to
assist the members in developing their own independence, the
pastor or leader unfortunately may pull out too early—before the
carers have solidified their skills and their confidence in offering
pastoral care. If a pastor's lack of involvement comes from a hesitancy to refer people in need to the lay pastoral carers for visits
and other kinds of involvement, the laity not only are prevented
from practicing their skills of visitation, they also receive an un-
spoken message that the pastor lacks trust in their ability to minister.

One danger the lay pastoral carers will have to guard against is
becoming an in-group. Exclusivity has occurred in other groups—
prayer circles, glossolalia (speaking in tongues) clusters, social
action task forces, and sharing or encounter groups within the
church. A subtle sense of being better than others can lead to this
end. Any "holier-than-thou" attitude among the lay pastoral carers,

however slight, will destroy the credibility and efficacy of the care they give.

Another potential problem for lay pastoral carers is burnout. Much has been written in recent years about this phenomenon among helping professionals as well as among students, volunteers, and other high achievers. Articles have also noted it among clergy and indicated that the extensive amount of time they give to caring for others' problems lends itself to burnout. It can happen to lay ministers as well. In their zeal to be helpful or their commitment to care (or even their avoidance of problems elsewhere in their lives), they can take on too much, burn out, and eventually drop out of the group or even the church.

It is important for the pastor and lay leader to be watchful for burnout. The person who is always available and never says no, who makes good visits and can always be counted on, may be the most likely candidate. Monthly meetings of the caregivers will provide support and a chance to share potentially burnt-out feelings.

One more difficulty that may arise is caused by the chronically needy person who latches onto a lay pastoral carer (or a series of them) and takes increasingly large amounts of her or his time. Frequently such people do not really want to bring any change to their lives but live perpetually and neurotically from crisis to crisis—and want to talk to *everyone* about *all* of them!

It is good for the pastor or consultant to intervene and draw up some guidelines for responding to the chronically dependent individual. The whole lay pastoral care group should be made aware of the plan of action so that the individual who does not get what she or he wants with one carer will not start the same process with another. Such planning frequently helps to prevent over-involvement with the chronic—but is not likely to solve the person's problem. Sometimes change will occur only when a major crisis hits, and the individual is forced by the situation to cope actively.

Most pastors know before referral which people in the congregation are potential chronics. If such a person is assigned only to an experienced lay pastoral carer who is warned of the situation, many future problems can be forestalled.

Advanced Training

The paradigm presented in this book is a basic training program for lay pastoral care. It is deliberately introductory and is by design quite different from an advanced program that would train pastors in chaplaincy or pastoral counseling. If an ongoing group is started at the end of the course to make visits for the church, further training would be beneficial.

Most churches (except very large congregations) will not be able to offer extended advanced training, but such training is not the only option. Lay pastoral carers, especially those in or near metropolitan areas, will have opportunities to attend seminars on a variety of subjects—grief, rape, parenting, and so on. Some of these programs are offered for mental health professionals only; others are open to nurses, teachers, police officers, and others. Additional sources for advanced training are the courses sponsored by crisis lines, information and referral services, rape counseling groups, and the like. Although of variable quality, such programs can be especially useful since they are geared to the nonprofessional helper. A number of seminaries, like my own, are offering courses (even degrees) for lay persons who want to learn more about the church and deepen their commitment to its ministry. Any additional training tends to heighten interest in lay pastoral care and increase confidence on the part of the caregiver.

Consultation

An ongoing program of consultation for lay pastoral carers is vital to their ministry. Ronald Sunderland, commenting on his observations of a number of different lay pastoral care programs, puts it this way, "The primary reason for the failure of many evangelism projects and lay pastoral care ministries in congregations has been the reluctance or inability of clergy to initiate rigorous supervision of lay ministers. The best training methods and materials available will represent wasted efforts—and money—if continuing, consistent oversight is not introduced at the outset."[2]

In spite of the new vocabulary of skills and increased self-confidence in helping others, lay pastoral carers usually will need to sense the support of the minister and the larger church and the security of knowing that, if they do get in over their heads, there will be someone available to offer unbiased feedback and even to intervene if necessary. The weight of responsibility for another's life or soul—or even well-being—is too great for one human to bear alone.

Monthly meetings of the caregivers, as described in chapter 3, will provide much of the needed consultation. The pastor or a skilled mental health professional within or without the congregation who volunteers to participate faithfully can provide specialized information and professional assistance. In addition, members of the group will become consultants for each other, lending emotional support and the objective third-party stance that is so needed in a situation of complex or disturbing emotions.

It may also be necessary for the minister to give individual supervision to caregivers—especially when they are grappling with unusually troubling or complicated situations. In these individual sessions it is possible to deal with the lay person's own personal problems or limitations and confront any irresponsible or thoughtless behavior on the caregiver's part.

Finally, it is a good and essential thing to reach beyond the immediate congregation as soon as the lay caregivers' group is fairly stable. Within every community there are countless institutions and individuals in desperate need of the redeeming force of God's love as channeled through God's people: psychiatric hospitals, a battered child, a battering parent, girls' clubs and boys' clubs, halfway houses, disabled vets, the lonely widower down the street, a business executive struggling for survival, alcoholism treatment centers, a gifted child, the community's public schools, a homemaker who has lost her dreams. Pastoral care is not meant only for "God's in-group"—the congregation—but it is also a part of the church's total mission of evangelism and outreach to the community and to the world.

Seminars and advanced training, consultation and supervision, outreach to the community—all contribute to the strength of a church's total lay pastoral care program and to its continued growth and service.

The subject of this book is nothing new to the church. Lay pastoral care has always been an integral part of our Christian history and tradition. It is, simply, our response to others out of love—and out of gratitude for the love so graciously given us by God. Only one task among many in the church, it joins with the ministries of music, of teaching, typing, preaching, cooking, writing, planning, sweeping, bookkeeping, reading and serving in which all of us (lay and clergy alike) participate. The human needs addressed by a pastoral care ministry are great; but equally great is the wealth of resources for caregiving among the members of the body of Christ.

Appendix A:
Affirming Your Own
Gifts

1 Corinthians 12:1-11

In this passage the Apostle Paul reminds the readers that each Christian has been given a unique set of "gifts" unlike anyone else. Not everyone's gifts are preaching, leadership and biblical interpretation. What are your gifts? Write down five specific gifts you have, and list examples of how you have used these gifts in the past.

1. Gift: _____

   Examples: _____

   _____

2. Gift: _____

   Examples: _____

   _____

3. Gift: _____

   Examples: _____

   _____

4. Gift: _____

   Examples: _____

   _____

5. Gift: _____

   Examples: _____

   _____

Appendix B: A Service for Commissioning Lay Pastoral Carers

PRESENTER: Pastor _____, the following persons have spent considerable time together learning some of the arts of the church's ministry of pastoral care: [*read names of lay pastoral carers*].

They have combined reading and discussion with visiting members and friends of this congregation to prepare for their formal recognition as lay pastoral carers.

They will continue to work together as a group to further their skills and experience in ministry, and will continue to support one another in this work.

I am pleased to present to you these men and women for commissioning as pastoral carers to minister to the homebound, the hospitalized, the institutionalized, and those in special need, and to bring the consecrated elements of the Holy Eucharist to those who cannot join us in worship.

PASTOR: One of the identifying marks of the Reformation was the reaffirmation of the priesthood or ministry of all believers. Today we are living out another chapter in that affirmation by commissioning you to assist the pastor(s) and this congregation in our ministry of pastoral care.

Already the impact of your ministry has been felt through your training, and I look forward to its continued effect. You, and the congregation, should know that the work of the pastoral carers is in addition to, not a substitute for, the pastoral care of your clergy.

I ask each of you now, having given yourself to the study and experience of the ministry of pastoral care: Do you willingly present yourselves before God and your congregation for commissioning?

LAY CARERS: We do.

PASTOR: Do you pledge to the best of your ability, acknowledging the guidance of the Spirit, to seek to heal, guide, sustain, and reconcile those given to your care?

LAY CARERS: We do.

PASTOR: Do you intend to continue your study, your growth, and your support of one another in your ministry?

LAY CARERS: We do.

PASTOR: Will the members of _____Church please rise. *[The pastoral carers face the congregation.]* You have heard these men and women state their pledge and intention for their ministry among and with us. Do you accept them as your pastoral care assistants, and will you support their ministry with prayer, with action, with curiosity, and with encouragement?

CONGREGATION: We do so intend. *[The congregation is seated and the lay pastoral carers turn to the pastor.]*

PASTOR: Having now heard your pledge and your intention, and having heard the support and affirmation of the members of this congregation, I joyfully commission each of you as a lay assistant into the pastoral care ministry of _____ Church. In the name of the Father, and of the Son, and of the Holy Spirit. Amen.

ALL: Our gracious God, you have called and you know each of us by name. Your good word to us is that you love each one of us. Bless richly, we pray, the ministry of these men and women. May a full measure of your power and your presence be their special gift, so that they might minister with joy, and caring, and gentleness, and firmness.

Even as we set aside these men and women for ministry, let none of us be misled into the belief that they are doing our work. We have all been called by you. Lead us each into our special ministry.

We pray believing in your power, your love, and your presence. Amen.

This order for a service commissioning lay pastoral carers (reproduced with minor changes) was written by the Reverend Robert W. Wohlfort, Ph.D., and was first used at the Lutheran Church of Saint Andrew, Silver Spring, Maryland. It may be used as is or adapted to the needs and usage of other congregations.

Appendix C:
Four Case Studies

Case studies provided by the pastor of a mainline Protestant church in a central Texas metropolitan area are presented here. Each group is assigned one of these cases. First read over the case and think of how you can respond to the people in the situation using your own gifts. Then discuss as a group how various members of the church (pastors and laypersons) can minister to them. Be creative. Think of ways each of you in the group can address their spiritual, physical, and emotional needs at this time.

Case #1

Janet, a homemaker (thirty-eight), and George, an engineer (thirty-nine), have been married for sixteen years and have two children: A boy, fourteen and a girl, eleven. The four of them have been active members of the church for three and a half years. Janet and George get divorced.

George's attendance at church drops dramatically. Soon people realize they have only seen him twice in the four months since the divorce. Janet remains active in the church. She is experiencing difficulties being a single parent of two children and holding down a new full-time job. The fourteen-year-old has been cutting classes at school.

Case #2

Ben (twenty-nine) and Lucy (twenty-seven) have been married for seven years and have two daughters, ages five and three. They have always been members of the church, though never very active.

Ben has performed well in his work (business management) and is rewarded with a significant promotion. Combining both of their salaries they are able to purchase a $280,000 home and several other things they have desired (a boat and two new cars). As a result of these purchases, things are tight financially.

With the promotion, Ben works long hours. Ben and Lucy co-teach the third and fourth grade Church School class, but recently he has been too busy to teach with her. He consistently eats dinner at the office and comes home late. Lucy and the children miss him. Lucy is irritated that he is "never home" and even wonders if his being gone all the time is all work.

Case #3

William (forty-seven) and Harriet (forty-nine) have been members of the church for eighteen years. Harriet dies of cancer.

The church responds beautifully to William during Harriet's illness and after her death. It has been three years now since Harriet died. William has not remarried. He has remained somewhat active in the church. At times he appears very depressed. He doesn't seem to be his old cheerful self. At other times, he seems irritable and his closest friends say they feel "cut off" from him. He regularly expresses to anyone who will listen his disssatisfaction with the general direction the church is going.

Case #4

Helen (eighty-two) has belonged to the church for over forty years. When she was able to get around she was a very active church member, holding a number of key positions of leadership in the congregation. She has not been able to attend church for almost ten years.

Helen has two children and many grandchildren and great-grandchildren. Her husband died over twenty years ago and her children moved away after graduating from college. She has no family who live nearby and few of her friends are able to visit her any more.

Helen refuses to go to a nursing home or retirement community, as her children have urged, but finds herself unable to leave her house very often. She relies upon a neighbor to do her shopping and on visits from family to keep the house up. She is lonely, somewhat forgetful, and has lost touch with most everyone in the church.

Notes

Preface

1. Howard Stone, *Suicide and Grief* (Philadelphia: Fortress Press, 1972), p. 108.
2. William A. Clebsch and Charles R. Jaekle, *Pastoral Care in Historical Perspective* (New York: Jason Aronson, 1964), p. 5.

Chapter 1

1. Clebsch and Jaekle, *Pastoral Care in Historical Perspective,* p. 4. Note: Throughout the book I use the terms *troubled person, distressed, individual with a problem,* and so on. These phrases are used for ease of presentation, but it should be stressed that pastoral care involves care offered not only to people with problems, but also to those desirous of personal or spiritual growth. In this regard Howard Clinebell (in personal correspondence) adds a fifth task to Clebsch and Jaekle's historical definition of pastoral care: nurturing growth and wholeness. The person who wants to deepen a faith relationship with God is just as important as the individual who is recovering a sense of meaning after the death of a spouse. As Brister has noted, "That care which distinguishes a true church of the living God from cults, esoteric sects, and other social groups is the profound concern for the total range of man's existence which pervades its life. Unlike some institutions of the community which are concerned with limited aspects of existence—education, health, welfare, and so on—the Christian congregation cherishes man in the totality of his life" (C.W. Brister, *Pastoral Care in the Church* [New York: Harper & Row, 1964], p. 23).
2. Clebsch and Jaekle, *Pastoral Care in Historical Perspective,* pp. 4–5.
3. Daniel Day Williams, *The Minister and the Care of Souls* (New York: Harper & Bros., 1961), p. 146.
4. Diane Detwiler-Zapp and William C. Dixon, *Lay Caregiving* (Philadelphia: Fortress Press, 1982), pp. 5–6.
5. For further discussion see my book, *Word of God and Pastoral Care* (Nashville: Abingdon Press, 1988); Clebsch and Jaekle, *Pastoral Care in Historical Perspective;* or Marcus Bryant, *The Art of Christian Caring* (St. Louis: Bethany Press, 1979), especially pp. 9–24.
6. Bryant, *Art of Christian Caring,* p. 24.
7. Detwiler-Zapp and Dixon, *Lay Caregiving,* pp. 10–11.

Chapter 2

1. Martin Luther, *Martin Luther: Selections from His Writings*, edited by John Dillenberger (New York: Doubleday Anchor, 1961), p. 53.
2. Paul Althaus, *The Ethics of Martin Luther*, translated by Robert C. Schultz (Philadelphia: Fortress Press, 1972), p. 6.
3. Althaus, *Ethics of Martin Luther*, pp. 14–15.
4. In discussing the law of love, I am not trying to detail a total ethic. For example, there is no attempt to address the ethical distinction between meeting the neighbor's *needs* and doing what the neighbor *desires*; that would be beyond the scope of this book. Rather, the aim is to articulate one part of an ethic that relates to pastoral care. For additional material the reader is referred to works such as Paul Althaus, *The Ethics of Martin Luther;* George W. Forell, *Christian Social Teachings* (New York: Doubleday Anchor, 1966); William Lazareth, *Luther on the Christian Home* (Philadelphia: Muhlenberg Press, 1960); Paul Lehmann, *Ethics in a Christian Context* (New York: Harper & Row, 1963); and others.
5. Victor Furnish, *The Love Command in the New Testament* (Nashville: Abingdon, 1972), pp. 44–45.
6. The "law of Christ" (Gal. 6:2), the "principle of faith" (Rom. 3:27), and the "law of the Spirit of life in Christ Jesus" (Rom. 8:2) are possible references to the dual love command.
7. Martin Luther, *Works of Martin Luther*, edited by Henry Jacobs (Philadelphia: 1915–1943), vol. 2, pp. 342–43.
8. Martin Luther, *D. Martin Luthers Werke*, edited by J. K. F. Kraake et al., Kritische Gesamtausgabe (Weimar: Bohlaus Nachfolger, 1883–   ), vol. 17:II, p. 99.
9. Luther, Weimar edition, vol. 8, p. 588.
10. Luther, Philadelphia edition, vol. 2, p. 335.
11. Luther, Weimar edition, vol. 10:III, p. 249.
12. Søren Kierkegaard, *Works of Love*, translated by David F. Swenson and Lillian M. Swenson (Princeton: Princeton University Press, 1949), p. 18.
13. See Ernst Käsemann, "Paul and Early Catholicism," in *New Testament Questions of Today*, translated by W. J. Montague and W. F. Bunge (Philadelphia: Fortress Press, 1969), pp. 246–47; or Herman G. Steumpfle, Jr., "Theological and Biblical Perspectives on the Laity" (pamphlet published by the Lutheran Church in America, Division for Mission in North America, 1973).
14. Alan Richardson, *An Introduction to the Theology of the New Testament* (New York: Harper & Bros., 1958), pp. 301–02.
15. Stuempfle, "Perspectives on the Laity," p. 6.
16. Quoted in ibid.
17. Accepting one's lot does not mean, as some have maintained, that certain people (such as women, blacks, or the handicapped) are therefore to be exploited and held in their place by the prevailing establishment. Each person has the responsibility to determine what can and cannot be changed.
18. Thomas G. Wilkens, "Ministry, Vocation, and Ordination: Some Perspectives from Luther," *The Lutheran Quarterly* 29 (Fall 1977), pp. 75–76.

19. *Luther's Works*, American Edition, edited by Jaroslav Pelikan and Helmut Lehmann (Philadelphia and St. Louis: Concordia Publishing House, 1955–), vol. 36, p. 116.
20. Quoted in Paul Althaus, *The Theology of Martin Luther*, translated by Robert C. Schultz (Philadelphia: Fortress Press, 1966), p. 314.

Chapter 4

1. Time estimates are presented to give the reader a sense of what portion of the training session is to be devoted to each segment. The time allotments can, of course, be varied to suit the leader's preference.
2. After each session a homework assignment is proposed, usually a suggestion for further reflection on the content of the class or to practice some of the skills taught that day. Homework does not have to be used as part of the program, but when it is, it is beneficial to spend a few minutes during the following session discussing the assignment.
3. Such as Matt. 22:34 ff., 25:35 ff.; Luke 10:25 ff.; John 13:34 ff., 20:21 ff.; Rom. 13:8-10; Gal. 6:2; 1 Cor. 12:1 ff.; James 1:27; 1 Pet. 2:9 ff.
4. See Howard W. Stone, *Crisis Counseling* (Philadelphia: Fortress Press, 1976), pp. 32–48.

Chapter 5

1. See Robert R. Carkhuff, *Helping and Human Relations*, 2 vols. (New York: Holt, Rinehart and Winston, 1969); Gerard Egan, *The Skilled Helper* (Monterey, Ca.: Brooks/Cole, 1990); Jerome D. Frank, *Persuasion and Healing* (New York: Schocken Books, 1961); Frederick H. Kanfer and Arnold P. Goldstein, eds., *Helping People Change* (New York: Pergamon Press, 1980); Carl R. Rogers, *Client-Centered Therapy* (Boston: Houghton Mifflin, 1951).
2. Arnold P. Goldstein, "Relationship-Enhancement Models," in Kanfer and Goldstein, eds., *Helping People Change*, p. 19.
3. Dietrich Bonhoeffer, *Life Together*, translated by John W. Doberstein (New York: Harper & Bros., 1954), p. 97.

Chapter 6

1. For additional help in do's and don'ts of responding, see Lewis R. Wolberg, *The Technique of Psychotherapy*, vol. 1, 3rd ed. (New York: Grune and Stratton, 1977), pp. 499–503.

Chapter 7

1. Rudolph E. Grantham, *Lay Shepherding: A Guide for Visiting the Sick, the Aged, the Troubled, and the Bereaved* (Valley Forge, Pa.: Judson Press, 1980), p. 46.
2. Ibid., p. 50.

Chapter 8

1. "The Death of a Wished-for Child" is distributed by the Order of the Golden Rule; "Begin with Goodbye: A Time to Cry" by Mass Media Ministries; "When a Child Dies" by the National Funeral Directors Association; and "Where Is Dead?" by the Encyclopaedia Britannica Educational Corporation.

2. David W. Berge and George B. Daugherty, *Death Education: Audio-Visual Sourcebook* (DeKalb, Ill.: Educational Perspectives Associates, 1976).
3. The National Research and Information Center, 1614 Central Street, Evanston, Ill. 60201. Volume 2, no. 5, of the *National Reporter* from the National Research and Information Center reviews a number of films.
4. See Edgar N. Jackson, *Understanding Grief* (New York: Abingdon, 1958); Kenneth R. Mitchell and Herbert Anderson, *All Our Losses, All Our Griefs: Resources for Pastoral Care* (Philadelphia: Westminster Press, 1983); Stone, *Suicide and Grief;* Scott Sullender, *Grief and Growth* (Mahwah, NJ: Paulist Press, 1985); David K. Switzer, *The Dynamics of Grief* (Nashville: Abingdon, 1970); and Granger E. Westberg, *Good Grief* (Philadelphia: Fortress Press, 1971); and others.
5. See Stone, *Suicide and Grief.*

Chapter 9

1. A note to leaders: some class members will not have completed their calls. Rather than criticizing them, see if anything can be done to help (to get up their courage, arrange their schedules, etc.) and urge them to do their visits in the coming week. Take note of individuals who are having obvious problems and talk with them privately after class. Participants who have already made calls, or other experienced lay carers in the congregation, may be used to accompany those class members during the first few visits.
2. See my book, *Word of God and Pastoral Care* (Nashville: Abingdon, 1988), chapter 3.
3. See Stone, *Crisis Counseling,* p. 20.
4. See William Countryman, *The Bible: Authority for Christian Pilgrimage* (Philadelphia: Fortress Press, 1982), chapter 1.
5. Martin Luther, *Luther's Prayers,* edited by Herbert F. Brokering (Minneapolis: Augsburg, 1967), p. 105.
6. For further resources see Charles Kemp, "Developing Spiritual Resources" (a pamphlet published by The United Christian Missionary Society, no date); or Kemp's *Learning About Pastoral Care* (New York: Abingdon, 1970), pp. 310–11; or Donald Capps, *Biblical Approaches to Pastoral Counseling* (Philadelphia: Fortress Press, 1981).

Chapter 10

1. For example, see Robert R. Carkhuff, *The Art of Problem Solving* (Amherst, Mass.: Human Resource Development Press, 1973); Jay Haley, *Problem-Solving Therapy: New Strategies for Effective Family Therapy* (San Francisco: Jossey-Bass, 1976); Egan, *The Skilled Helper,* pp. 182–232; and Howard W. Stone, *Using Behavioral Methods in Pastoral Counseling* (Philadelphia: Fortress Press, 1980), pp. 70–74.
2. O. Hobart Mowrer, quoted in Howard J. Clinebell, Jr., *Basic Types of Pastoral Counseling* (Nashville: Abingdon Press, 1966), p. 171.
3. Marcus Bryant and Charles Kemp, *The Church and Community Resources* (St. Louis: Bethany Press, 1977).

Chapter 11

1. For further reading concerning assessment of suicide lethality, see especially Norman L. Farberow, Samuel M. Heilig, and Robert E. Litman, *Techniques in Crisis Intervention: A Training Manual* (Los Angeles: Suicide Prevention Center, 1968); or Stone, *Suicide and Grief*, pp. 15–20.
2. The author would appreciate knowing any changes you have found helpful in the training you do. Send them to Brite Divinity School, Texas Christian University, P.O. Box 32923, Fort Worth, Texas 76129.

Chapter 12

1. Furnish, *The Love Command*, p. 196.
2. Ronald D. Sunderland, "Lay Pastoral Care," *The Journal of Pastoral Care* 42 (Summer 1988), pp. 169–70.

For Further Reading

Althaus, Paul. *The Ethics of Martin Luther.* Translated by Robert C. Schultz. Philadelphia: Fortress Press, 1972.

_____. *The Theology of Martin Luther.* Translated by Robert C. Schultz. Philadelphia: Fortress Press, 1966.

Ammons, Edsel. "Clergy and Laity: Equally Called." *Christian Century* 92 (February 5–12, 1975), pp. 107–109.

Ayres, Francis O. *The Ministry of the Laity: A Biblical Exposition.* Philadelphia: Westminster Press, 1962.

Barr, Browne, and Eakin, Mary. *The Ministering Congregation.* Philadelphia: United Church Press, 1972.

Bovet, Theodore. *That They May Have Life.* Translated by John A. Baker. London: Darton, Longman & Todd, 1964.

Brister, C.W. *People Who Care.* Nashville: Broadman Press, 1967.

Brown, G. , Jr. "Towards More Effective Ministry Through Communities of Enabling." *Reform Review* 27 (Fall 1973), pp. 41–49.

Bryant, Marcus D. *The Art of Christian Caring.* St. Louis: The Bethany Press, 1979.

Bryant, Marcus D., and Kemp, Charles F. *The Church and Community Resources.* St. Louis: The Bethany Press, 1977.

Butt, Howard, and Wright, Elliott. *At the Edge of Hope.* New York: Seabury Press, 1978.

Campbell, Alastair V. *Professionalism and Pastoral Care.* Philadelphia: Fortress Press, 1985.

Carkhuff, Robert R. *The Art of Helping.* Amherst, Mass.: Human Resource Development Press, 1972.

_____. *The Art of Problem Solving.* Amherst, Mass.: Human Resource Development Press, 1973.

Clinebell, Howard. "How to Set Up and Lead a Grief Recovery Group." *Christian Ministry* 6 (November 1975), pp. 34–36.

Cougar, Yves Marie Joseph. *Lay People in the Church.* Westminster, Md.: Newman Press, 1965.

Detwiler-Zapp, Diane, and Dixon, William C. *Lay Caregiving.* Philadelphia: Fortress Press, 1982.

Dicks, Russell L. *How to Make Pastoral Calls: A Guide for Laymen.* St. Louis: The Bethany Press, 1962.

Egan, Gerard. *The Skilled Helper.* Pacific Grove, Ca.: Brooks/Cole Publishing, 1990.

Feucht, Oscar E. *Everyone a Minister.* St. Louis: Concordia Publishing House, 1977.

Furnish, Victor Paul. *The Love Command in the New Testament.* Nashville: Abingdon Press, 1972.

Grantham, Rudolph E. *Lay Shepherding: A Guide for Visiting the Sick, the Aged, the Troubled, and the Bereaved.* Valley Forge, Pa.: Judson Press, 1980.

Hall, Cameron P. *Lay Action: The Church's Third Force.* New York: Friendship Press, 1974.

Haugk, Kenneth C. *Christian Caregiving: A Way of Life.* Minneapolis: Augsburg, 1984.

Hinand, A. J. "Pastor as Enabler for Lay Ministry." *Pastoral Psychology* 22 (June 1971), pp. 21–26.

Johnson, Douglas W. *The Care and Feeding of Volunteers.* Nashville: Abingdon Press, 1978.

Killinger, John. *The Tender Shepherd.* Nashville: Abingdon Press, 1985.

Kromminga, Carl Gerhard. *The Communication of Gospel Through Neighboring.* Netherlands: T. Wever, 1964.

Kuhn, Barbara. *The Whole Lay Ministry Catalogue.* New York: Seabury Press, 1979.

Lindgren, Alvin J., and Shawchuck, Norman. *Let My People Go: Empowering Laity for Ministry.* Nashville: Abingdon Press, 1980.

Luther, Martin. *Luther's Works.* General editors Jaroslav Pelikan (vols. 1–30) and Helmut Lehmann (vols. 31–55). Philadelphia: Fortress Press, and St. Louis: Concordia Publishing House, 1955–   .

Marney, Carlyle. *Priests to Each Other.* Valley Forge, Pa.: Judson Press, 1974.

Nouwen, Henri J.M.; McNeill, Donald P.; and Morrison, Douglas A. *Compassion: A Reflection on the Christian Life.* New York: Doubleday and Company, 1982.

Olson, Eldon L. "Lay Care Ministries: A Pastoral Theological Assessment." *Journal of Supervision and Training* 10 (1988), pp. 170–178.

Oglesby, William B. "Lay Pastoral Care Revisited." *The Journal of Pastoral Care* 40 (June 1986), pp. 119–128.

Raines, Robert A. *New Life in the Church.* New York: Harper & Row, 1961.

Schaller, Lyle E. *The Pastor and the People: Building a New Partnership for Effective Ministry.* Nashville: Abingdon Press, 1973.

Smith, Donald P. *Congregations Alive.* Philadelphia: Westminster Press, 1981.

_____. "Shared Ministry." *Theology Today* 36 (October 1979), pp. 338–46.

Southard, Samuel. *Comprehensive Pastoral Care.* Valley Forge, Pa.: Judson Press, 1975.

Sterner, R. Eugene. *You Have a Ministry.* Anderson, Ind.: Warner Press, 1963.

Stone, Howard W. *Crisis Counseling.* Philadelphia: Fortress Press, 1976.

_____. *Suicide and Grief.* Philadelphia: Fortress Press, 1972.

_____. *Using Behavioral Methods in Pastoral Counseling.* Philadelphia: Fortress Press, 1980.

_____. *Word of God and Pastoral Care.* Nashville: Abingdon Press, 1988.

Sullender, Scott. *Grief and Growth.* Mahwah, NJ: Paulist Press, 1985.

Sunderland, Ronald D. "Lay Pastoral Care." *The Journal of Pastoral Care* 42 (Summer 1988), pp. 159–171.

Van Wagner, Charles A., II. "Supervision of Lay Pastoral Care." *The Journal of Pastoral Care* 31 (September 1977), pp. 158–63.

Vos, Nelvin. *Monday's Ministries: The Ministry of the Laity.* Philadelphia: Parish Life Press, 1979.

Wentz, Frederick K. *The Layman's Role Today.* New York: Abingdon Press, 1980.

Wilke, Harold H. *Creating the Caring Congregation: Guidelines for Ministering with the Handicapped.* Nashville: Abingdon Press, 1980.